THE 250 BEST SHOP TRICKS

One of the best things that happens when a bunch of woodworkers get together is sharing shop secrets. You've got a great idea for getting more accurate cuts? I'll trade you for some of my hardware storage solutions!

Here at *Woodworker's Journal*, we're lucky enough to get a never-ending stream of these hints from our readers. We call them *Tricks of the Trade*, and we share them regularly in our magazine. We know how useful they are to our readers — so we decided to create an even better tool by putting over 250 of these tricks in one place!

Larry N. Stoiaken
Editor in Chief

WOODWORKER'S JOURNAL

Copyright © 2000 Rockler Press.

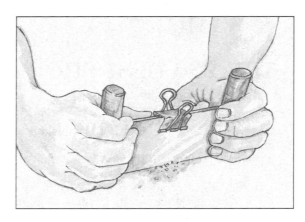

Q&A

"How do I stop sawdust from sticking to the gear and screw mechanism of my table saw?"

The answer, according to Walter France of Lithia Springs, Georgia, is to give the mechanism a thorough cleaning, then spray with silicone. This causes the dust to fall off instead of accumulating, and it also prevents rust.

A Simple Scraper Holder

This simple scraper holder consists of two dowels joined by a flexible piece of 1/8" plywood. A 1/4" slot is routed into each dowel and the dowels are then glued to the plywood. To achieve maximum flexibility, the plywood is cut so the exterior grain runs parallel to the dowels. The blade fits into the slots and is held by a binder clip.

A. M. Benson
Houston, Texas

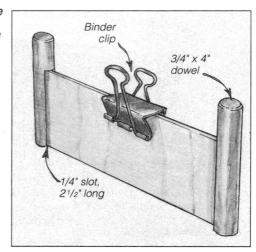

Binder clip

3/4" x 4" dowel

1/4" slot, 2¹/₂" long

The Half-lid Paint Striker

Next time you begin a paint job requiring a whole can of paint, remove the lid and use a hacksaw to cut it in two. Put one half aside for later, then slightly bend down the cut edge of the other and press it back in place atop the can. This half lid makes a sturdy brush shelf and the cut edge can be used to strike excess paint from the brush.

Lane Olinghouse
Everett, Washington

Bent down edge

Tape Measure Tip

The bulky case of a tape measure sometimes gets in the way in tight spots, so I kept a one-foot section of an old tape and ground both ends to make it accurate. I also made 24" and 36" measures this way — they work great inside cabinets.

Robert Guyan
Portland, Oregon

Quick Tip

Professional woodworkers generally keep their drawings and notes on a clipboard, but even then they get dog-eared and dirty. A piece of clear Plexiglas™, cut to 9" x 11" size, makes a great protector, but it also opens up a few other possibilities. By gluing a transparent ruler and protractor (both are available at office supply stores at very little cost) to the Plexiglas, you'll have an instant way to measure drawings, small parts and angles. Use a clear glue.

Q&A

"How do I straighten a warped board?"

If a board is warped along its edge, that's an easy fix. Simply run it across a jointer. If it's cupped across its width, you can try ripping it into two or even three narrow boards, jointing their edges, then reversing the grain in every other board when you glue them back together. Twisted stock is usually beyond help: your best bet may be to cut it up and use it where small parts are required.

There's a Hole in the Bucket ...

I put a plastic bag in my Shop-Vac to hold the dust so it would be easier to dump out. But the bag kept getting sucked up into the filter. So I found a pail that just fits inside the plastic bag, and I cut the bottom out. Now, I just take the pail out first and the bag comes out easily — and dust doesn't fly all over!

Arthur Duffie
Kalamazoo, Michigan

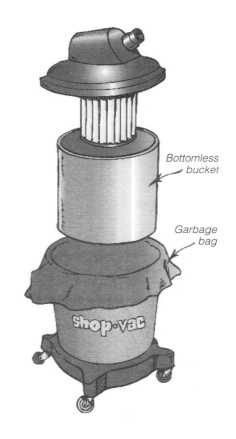

Bottomless bucket

Garbage bag

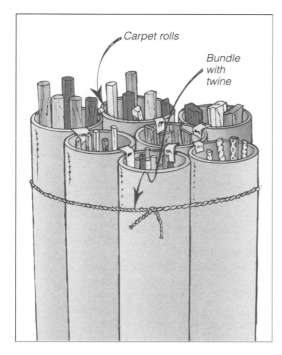

Carpet rolls

Bundle with twine

Quick Tip

A surface planer doesn't flatten boards. All it does is make them the same thickness along their length. If you feed a warped board through a planer, all you'll get at the other end is a uniformly thick warped board.

To get a flat board, first dress one face of the board on a jointer or a wide belt sander. Then lay the flattened (dressed) face on the planer bed, while the knives flatten the second face.

Small Stock Storage

Heavy cardboard carpet tubes (usually available FREE from a local carpet layer or store) can be cut to any length and bundled together with cord. Mine are 18" long, and I use them to separate different dowel scraps and leftover hardwood moldings. I can check my inventory at a glance: the tubes rest on the floor under my workbench, set on 2x4 scraps to keep them off the concrete. While tying the cord, use masking tape to temporarily hold them together (or you'll look like Charlie Chaplin chasing them all over!).

Barb Siddiqui
Wenatchee, Washington

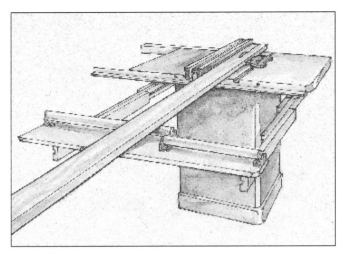

Q&A

"What do I do with a worn-out cordless drill battery?"

Ni-Cad (nickel-cadmium) batteries pose a serious threat to our groundwater, so they're not welcome at the landfill. Most cities have a system in place for dealing with them: call your courthouse or landfill office. Or call 800-8-BATTERY and get the name of a local retailer who will take them off your hands ... without a charge!

Sliding Supports

I use a pair of dining table slides and a couple of rollers to support long boards on my table saw (above). I attached the slides to the bottom of the saw's tabletop and mounted the rollers on a board stretched between them. When not in use, the slides can be pushed out of the way (below).

Robert Floyd
Hilton, New York

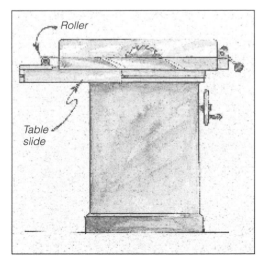

Roller

Table slide

8

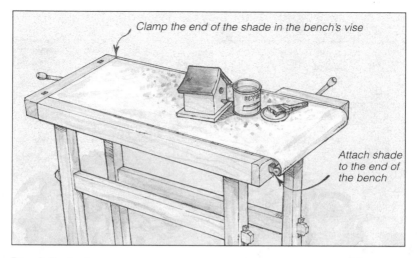

Clamp the end of the shade in the bench's vise

Attach shade to the end of the bench

Bench Protectors

To protect my maple workbench from paint or stain splatters, I mounted a white vinyl window shade roller to one end of the worktop. When I'm ready to finish, I just extend the shade across the bench. After the finish dries, the shade rolls out of the way. And the best part is that replacement shades are very inexpensive.

Robert O. Wendel
Marlboro, New Jersey

Wood Filler Woes

I wanted to avoid the inevitable blemishes that occur when excess wood filler surrounds nail heads in trim and moldings. So I came up with this idea: place a short piece of masking tape over the area around the nail head, then set the nail right through the tape. Apply the wood filler and, while it is still soft, peel off the tape. A perfect round spot is left, with no accumulation on the surrounding area.

James Vasi
Williamsville, New York

Quick Tip

Turners often leave a short log inside the bag on their dust collection system. The combination of flowing air, sawdust and chips tends to dry out the stock in an even, controlled fashion. But try it on a less favored piece first: results vary widely depending on how often the dust collector is used, the log species, the geographic location of the shop and the length of time the log is allowed to stay in the bag.

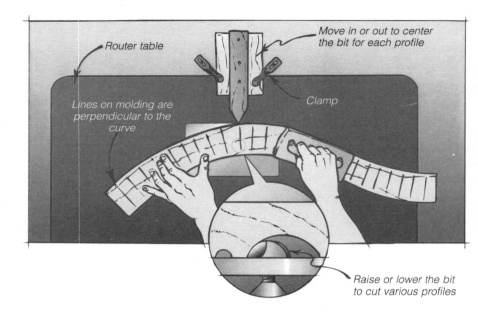

Router table

Move in or out to center the bit for each profile

Lines on molding are perpendicular to the curve

Clamp

Raise or lower the bit to cut various profiles

Q&A

"I use wood blocks to save the workpiece while I tighten clamps, but I run out of fingers trying to hold them in place. Any ideas?"

Kenneth J. Shaw of Holley, New York tells us that he attaches those scraps to the jaws of his clamps with hot melt glue, so they're removable when he's done.

S-shaped Moldings on a Router Table

None of my woodworking friends could advise me how to cut a profile down the middle of an S-shaped molding, so I came up with the solution shown here. After band-sawing and drum sanding the piece to shape, I made pencil marks every inch along the back of the workpiece. These were perpendicular to the curve (see drawing). Then I clamped a pointed guide fence to the router table that centered the bit where I wanted it, set my bit height, and started running the piece through the cutter. By adjusting the work so that the pencil lines were always at 90° to the fence, I kept the cut in line. A little carving and sanding smoothed out any rough spots.

G. R. Williams
Fostoria, Ohio

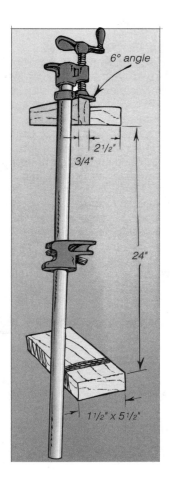

6° angle

2¹/₂"

3/4"

24"

1¹/₂" x 5¹/₂"

Quick Tip

Hammering small nails can be a real challenge, especially if you have large fingers. One way to deal with the problem is to stick the nail through a piece of paper, then use the paper to hold it in place while you start driving it. Once the nail is secure, the paper just pulls away. Craig Kimpston of Grimes, Iowa, has a more innovative method: he uses the teeth on his pocket comb to hold nails while he starts them.

Three-piece Clamp Hanger

Storing pipe clamps has always been a challenge for me. I think I've contemplated every system in the world. Quite by accident, I stumbled on the method shown here. It requires only three pieces of wood assembled with drywall screws.

Michael Burton
Ogden, Utah

Q&A

An Extra Vise for your Shop

While working on a project requiring hand-cut dovetails, I came up with this simple vise idea. I took a scrap of hardwood 1" thick by 18" long by 8" wide and predrilled and countersunk holes 1" from the top edge. Then I cut a slot on both ends, 3" deep and wide enough to accommodate my Bessey bar clamps. I took a second piece the same size and cut the slots in the same place. Then I fastened the first piece to the workbench, slid in the clamps, and put the second piece on with the screw ends facing out. Now I have an extra wood vise whenever I need one.

Pat Pelkey
Oswego, New York

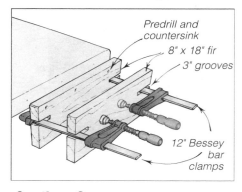

Predrill and countersink

8" x 18" fir

3" grooves

12" Bessey bar clamps

Creating a Curve

To draw a curve, compress a thin strip of wood between the jaws of a bar clamp. The clamp threads allow micro-adjustments of the curve.

William Adsit
Milford, Illinois

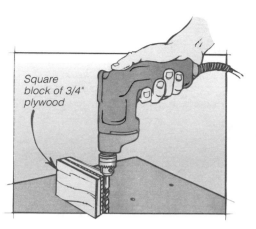

Square block of 3/4" plywood

Quick Tip

If you're getting a little tearout or feathering on boards as you run them across the jointer, try reversing the direction of the feed. Sometimes, grain hits the knives at the wrong angle. By switching the front of the board to the back, you offer a different grain angle to the cutters. If the knives are nicked, just loosen one and move it left or right, as far as it will go. Leave the others as they are and you'll get clean, sharp cuts.

Keeping the Bit Perpendicular

I've seen many great tips on how to hold a hand drill at a right angle to your work surface — everything from mirrors to specially cut jigs. I just use a piece of 3/4" plywood cut at a right angle. The 90° angle keeps the drill bit straight one way, and I use the very visible glue lines in the plywood to keep the bit perpendicular the other way. It's always worked for me, and it's pretty convenient.

Henry R. Dillon
Riverdale, Georgia

Router Skid Marks

When trimming plastic laminate, avoid black marks left by the router sub-base by occasionally spraying with WD40. This will also lubricate the bearing. (You shouldn't use oil on wood surfaces, though.)

Joe Nelson
S. CleElum, Washington

13

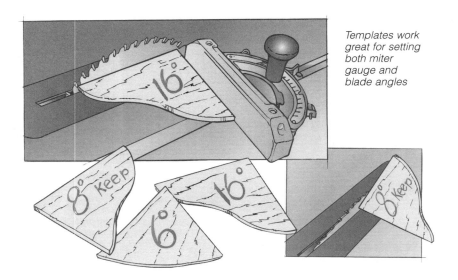

Templates work great for setting both miter gauge and blade angles

Q&A

"How do I remove water stains from a table?"

One of the most unusual and effective methods we've heard about (but never tried!) is to rub out the mark with standard mayonnaise! Apparently, mayo has just the right grit and chemical makeup to neutralize the blemish.

Table Saw Angles

Rather than look for a protractor or T-bevel, or trust the arrow indicators, I made a set of the angles I most commonly use to adjust my table saw and miter gauge. 1/4" plywood works fine for this. I use them again and again to set my saw for cutting angles, pentagons, hexagons, octagons and even segmented bowls.

Richard Dorn
Oelwein, Iowa

Toner Trick

When I need to transfer a pattern or drawing onto a piece of wood, I make a copy on a copy machine and iron it onto the wood. The heat from the iron transfers the toner onto the wood.

E. Frohnhoefer
Riverhead, New York

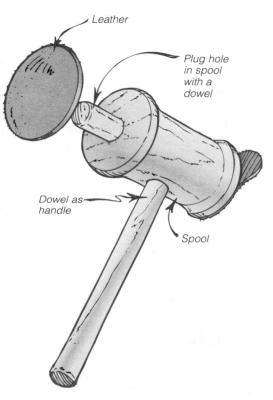

Leather

Plug hole
in spool
with a
dowel

Dowel as
handle

Spool

Quick Tip

Thread Spool: A Shop Aid

Sometimes, when doing light woodworking or model construction, a small wooden mallet is very handy. I found an empty thread spool made just such a mallet. First, I glued a section of dowel through the center hole of the spool and sanded this flush with the spool faces. Then I glued a leather disk to each of the faces. Next, I drilled a hole through the body of the spool and glued a short piece of dowel there to act as a handle. I have found this tool to be most useful for model work.

Howard E. Moody
Upper Jay, New York

15

Q&A

"What's the sequence for sanding grits?"

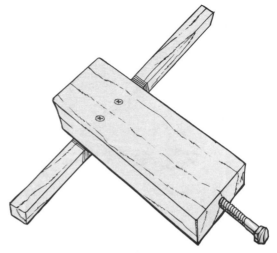

Most woodworking projects are sanded first with a 100 or 120 grit paper, then a 150. This is usually followed by 180 grit paper, then 220. After applying a first coat of finish (or a sanding seal coat), you can break it down with 280, 320 or 400 grit paper. The finest grade of over-the-counter paper is 800 grit, although finer polishing papers are available. At the other end of the scale, stock removal is done with coarse grits from 12 to 60.

Table Saw Alignment Jig

This little jig (above and below) slides in the miter gauge slot on my table saw and allows me to align the blade perfectly with the slot. To use it, I set the head of the bolt so it just barely grazes the saw blade at the front of the blade, as close to the teeth as possible. Then I slide it to the back of the blade and check again to see if any minor realignment is required.

Sean Bree
New York, New York

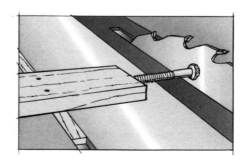

16

Duplicating Spindles

I made a bench with 13 spindles that had to be exact duplicates of each other, so I built a gauge by drilling several holes of varying sizes in a line along a piece of 1/4" hardboard. Then I ripped it down the middle. By marking the corresponding thicknesses on my turning blanks, I could simply stop the lathe, place my gauge on each of the marks and check my progress.

James A. Johnson
Brunswick, Ohio

Quick Tip

Keep a couple of hard-bristled toothbrushes handy in your shop and you'll find hundreds of uses for them. They're perfect for cleaning out carvings and intricate patterns when refinishing, or getting rid of dust and oil buildup on router bit bearings. They can be used to clean delicate parts where a wire brush would be too intrusive or coarse. And nothing works like a toothbrush and an air gun to clear dust from an inside corner before finishing.

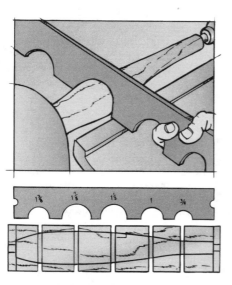

A Razor Edge on Turning Tools

Use a felt-tipped pen to coat the entire cutting edge of a tool and see how you're progressing while you sharpen it.

Howard Moody
Upper Jay, New York

Q&A

"How do I stop tearout in the underside of a veneered plywood sheet, when cross-cutting it on the table saw?"

By cutting it twice! The first time through, set the blade height at 1/8", then make the cut slowly with a sharp, multi-tooth (at least 60 teeth) blade. Then raise the blade and make the second cut all the way through. This method will eliminate almost all tearout problems. Putting masking tape along the cut line also helps a little.

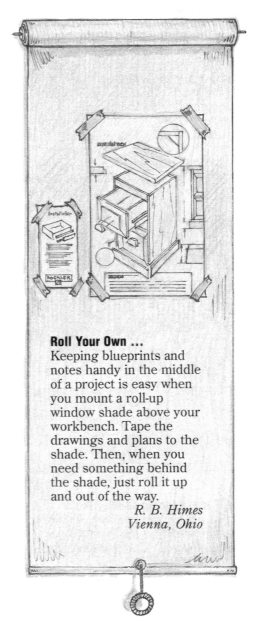

Roll Your Own ...
Keeping blueprints and notes handy in the middle of a project is easy when you mount a roll-up window shade above your workbench. Tape the drawings and plans to the shade. Then, when you need something behind the shade, just roll it up and out of the way.
R. B. Himes
Vienna, Ohio

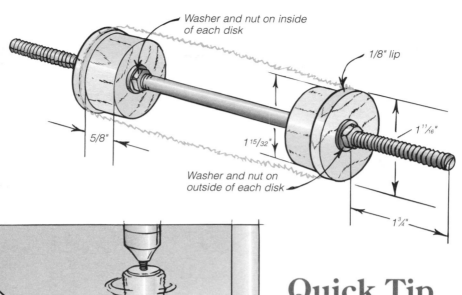

Washer and nut on inside of each disk

1/8" lip

5/8"

1 15/32"

1 11/16"

Washer and nut on outside of each disk

1 3/4"

Quick Tip

Build a Small Parts Buffer

Mount half a paint roller in your drill press or lathe to buff small parts. To do so, turn two 3/4" disks for the ends, leaving a 1/8" lip as shown above. Secure these on a length of threaded rod with nuts and bolts, spacing them just far enough apart to accept one half of a 9" long paint roller. Leave a couple of inches of rod for the chuck to bite. Clean the roller by wetting a cloth with paint thinner and holding it against the roller as it turns.

William Robidoux Jr.
Tiverton, Rhode Island

Q&A

"How can I flute dowels?"

Flutes are cut into dowels to allow excess glue and pockets of trapped air to escape as the dowel joint is clamped shut. Several manufacturers offer pre-fluted dowels, but you can make your own in a pinch. Just drag a length of dowel sideways across one tooth of a circular saw blade. Make sure the blade is secured (as in a vise), and keep your hands away from the teeth. Two flutes are usually more than adequate.

Drill bushings

4"

2 1/4"

3/4" x 3/4" guide rails

3 1/2"

3 3/4"

5"

5 1/2"

Drilling Center Holes

Here's an easy-to-build jig for drilling centered holes in round stock. The drill guide is a large block made by gluing up three pieces of stock, while the base is comprised of a glued up bottom, two ends and a pair of guide rails. Make sure the block moves freely in the base and use a slightly undersized bit when drilling holes for the 1/4", 5/16" and 3/8" ID bushings.

Salvatore F. Pontecorvo
Fort Wayne, Indiana

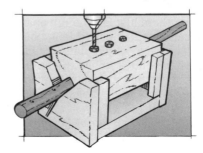

Shop Made Hold-downs

Here are two tricks to keep lumber tight to the saw tabletop (or a fence). The first is to cut a 30° kerf in a piece of plywood and insert a flexible putty knife, then clamp the unit to the fence. The second idea is a little more complex, as shown in the drawings below.

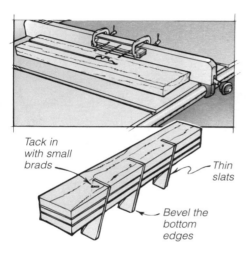

Tack in
with small
brads

Thin
slats

Bevel the
bottom
edges

This is a piece of 3/4" plywood with kerfs long enough to hold wooden slats like paint stirring paddles. Glue and tack the slats in place after beveling the bottoms for better contact with the wood. The hold-down can be made any length or width: longer models work wonderfully when you're ripping long stock on the table saw.

R.B.Himes
Vienna, Ohio

Quick Tip

Spline joints are a great way to join two long edges. But while most woodworkers have no problem routing the grooves for the spline, they often let the ball drop when it comes to making the actual spline. A ripped piece of hardwood won't work, as it will split along the grain — right where you need the most strength. Plywood is the perfect answer: its alternating grain prevents splitting, and it comes in thicknesses that are perfectly suited to the router bits you use to make the grooves.

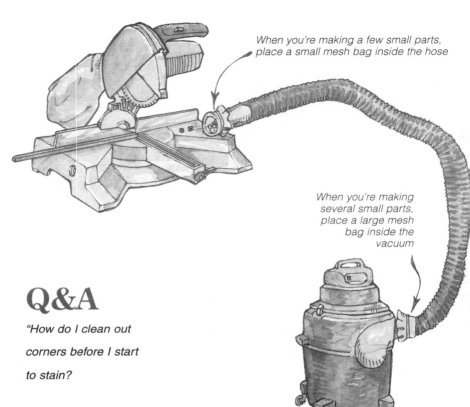

When you're making a few small parts, place a small mesh bag inside the hose

When you're making several small parts, place a large mesh bag inside the vacuum

Q&A

"How do I clean out corners before I start to stain?

Howard Moody of Upper Jay, New York, offers this simple solution: he buys a small whisk broom and reforms its flat bottom edge into a point. Howard tells us that his little custom brooms work great for those hard-to-reach corners, and they usually save him from dragging out the shop vacuum.

It's In the Bag
When cutting several small pieces on my miter or table saws, I put a mesh bag in the body of my shop vacuum and hold it in place with one end of the hose. I attach the other end of the hose close to my saw blade. When I turn on the vacuum and the saw, the vacuum pulls the sawdust into the body and the mesh bag traps the small pieces I'm making. If I only need a few parts, I put the mesh bag in the other end of the hose, near the saw.

Stanley A. Pulaski
Cedar Springs, Michigan

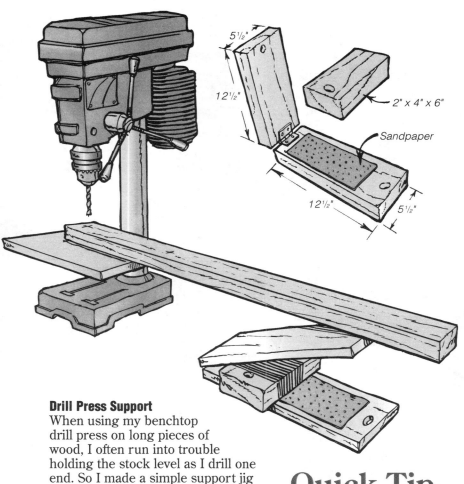

5½"

12½"

2" x 4" x 6"

Sandpaper

12½" 5½"

Drill Press Support

When using my benchtop drill press on long pieces of wood, I often run into trouble holding the stock level as I drill one end. So I made a simple support jig using two pieces of 3/4" plywood joined at one end with a butt hinge: this covers the full range of adjustment for my drill press table. A 6" long piece of scrap 2 x 4 serves as the adjusting block. It can be used flat or on edge, depending on the angle required. I glued a piece of medium grit sandpaper onto the lower flap of the jig, to keep the block from slipping when I put the weight of the stock on it.

Bob Kelland
Newfoundland, Canada

Quick Tip

When you spray lacquer in humid weather, a white blush reaction sometimes occurs. Roman Hershberger of Millersburg, Ohio, solves this problem by spraying a light mist of lacquer thinner on the blushing area.

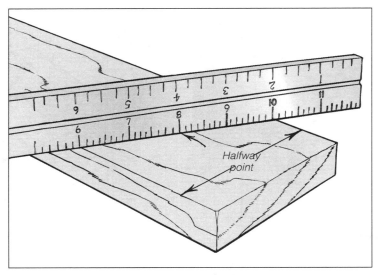

Halfway point

Q&A

"How do I avoid nicking the steel faceplate on my lathe when turning a bowl?"

Glue your turning blank to a disk of 3/4" thick wood the same diameter as the blank. (Insert a page of newspaper between them before you glue and clamp them together: this makes separation after turning a lot easier.) Then simply screw the disk to the steel faceplate.

Short Cut to the Center
Problem: find the center of a $5\,^9/_{16}$" wide board. Solution: Place a square at an angle on your board, with the inch marks on edge. Rotate the square until two numbers that are easily divided in half are on the edges (in this case, 6 and 10; so the center of our board is at the 8" mark).

Walter Keller
Fritch, Texas

Straighten out those Curves
It's difficult to cut a curved line perfectly and, if you have cut away your marks, it's almost impossible to find exactly where the irregularities are. Try stretching a thin piece of band steel (or even an old band saw blade) along the curve. The exact position and severity of any irregularities will become immediately apparent.

Michael Burton
Ogden, Utah

Storing Hand Planes

I wanted my hand planes to be within easy reach, but I also wanted to protect the cutting edges of their blades. So I built a modified tray that stores the planes right on my benchtop. The bottom is a scrap of plywood, and the sides are mitered stock left over from another project. Small strips of wood raise the fronts of the planes, keeping the blade edges clear of the bottom of the box. Angled strips underneath the tray prop up the entire assembly, and cross-strips stop the planes from sliding around, especially when I move the tray.

Kevin Hemmingsen
Wabasha, Minnesota

Quick Tip

If you like the look of Honduras mahogany, but feel the price is a little steep, consider substituting clear Spanish cedar. When finished clear, it is very similar to mahogany – just as rich and deep, with quite a bit of character, too. The cedar is available in fairly wide boards (not as wide as mahogany), and it is a little lighter in weight.

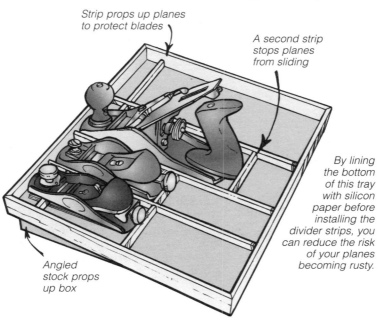

Strip props up planes to protect blades

A second strip stops planes from sliding

By lining the bottom of this tray with silicon paper before installing the divider strips, you can reduce the risk of your planes becoming rusty.

Angled stock props up box

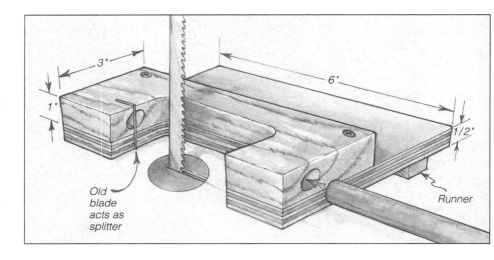

The illustration is labeled with: 3", 1", 6", 1/2", "Old blade acts as splitter", and "Runner"

Q&A

"How do I get rid of large quantities of sawdust?"

Anyone who owns large animals would be delighted to get your sawdust for bedding. Just be sure you let them know what species you've been milling, and have them call their vet to make sure there are no problems. For example, horses have been known to get cholic when exposed to some species like walnut.

No-Twist Dowel Splitting

To split dowels on my band saw, I use guide blocks with holes drilled for each size dowel. These blocks are screwed to 1/2" plywood bases. Make a 2" x 2" cutout in the jig, then draw a line through the dowel guide hole and make a 1/4" deep band saw cut. Epoxy part of an old band saw blade into the cut, to prevent your dowels from twisting. A runner attached to the bottom of the base runs in the miter gauge slot and guides your cut.

Don Kinnamon
Munds Park, Arizona

Anti-static Dust Sweeping

Spray a little Static Guard on a soft brush to clean up fine dust when you sand between coats of finish. A light coat is all you need: too much will interfere with the finish.

Roger Berg
Farmington, Wisconsin

Green Stock Dryer

Too busy to paint the ends of a piece of green stock, I just tossed it in a box of shavings and forgot about it for several days. When I returned to it, there wasn't a single check in the end. Sawdust seems to draw out the moisture at a fast rate with no checks and little warpage. After initial drying in the dust, you can remove the stock and let it air dry. Sticks work best with the bark off. Just stir up the shavings every day or two so the moisture doesn't accumulate and grow mildew.

Jeff Rose
Monticello, Minnesota

Flat Out Fabulous

When working on carpentry rather than furniture projects, there are two good reasons to trade in your standard #2 pencil for the traditional carpenters' variety. First, the flat ones won't roll off a slanted surface like a roof. Second, the chiseled end tends to hold an edge longer than a pared point.

John Tyler
Osceola, Wisconsin

Turners' Fast Finish

Need a fast satin finish? Apply wipe-on polyurethane with a paper towel and immediately wipe it off while the piece is still spinning. This creates enough heat to quickly set the poly and bring out a beautiful satin finish.

Ron Hampton
Texarkana, Texas

Quick Tip

When turning a lid for a vessel, it's a good idea to make it a little too tight to start with, then remove it from the lathe and shave wood a hair at a time with a sander, file or chisel, for a nice, tight fit. Make sure both the lid and the opening are fully dry (about 6% moisture), or one may shrink at a different rate than the other: in that case, the lid will either stick or fall out. Watch the grain direction, too. Wood moves across the grain a lot more than it does along the grain, so your lid may fit in one direction, but turn it 90° and see if it still does before putting your tools away.

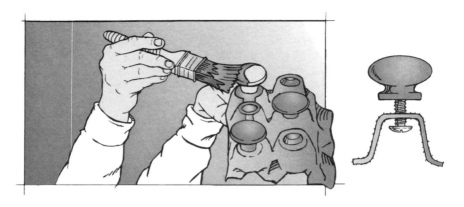

Q&A

"How do I space the boards

on my picnic table equally?"

One of the oldest tricks in

the shop is to drive a 16d

nail through a small block

of pine, then use this to

create equal spacing on

decks and outdoor furniture.

The diameter of the nail

produces roughly a 1/8"

gap, perfect for rain and

melting snow. The scrap

of wood straddles both

pieces of lumber as they're

being secured, freeing up

your hands.

Egg-cellent Solution ...

I use egg cartons to support knobs and such as I paint or finish them. Punch a small hole in the base of each recess in one half of a carton, then screw the knobs in place. Not only does this keep you and the workspace clean, it holds the knobs while they dry.

Margie Kelland
St. John's, Newfoundland

Stick Around

I have several stationary tools that need different wrenches to change bits or blades. I keep the right tool handy with large magnets from old stereo speakers.

Richard Irvine
Gibsons, British Columbia

Stick Around

I had a machine shop transform a $10 garage sale table saw (minus motor) into a router table with three steel inserts, and do it for just $85. The saw fence works great with the router.

Paul Dachel
Wisconsin Rapids, Wisconsin

Slick Solution

I polish my table saw's top with clear shoe polish. It completely eliminates resistance and doesn't stick to wood.

Roger Berg
Farmington, Wisconsin

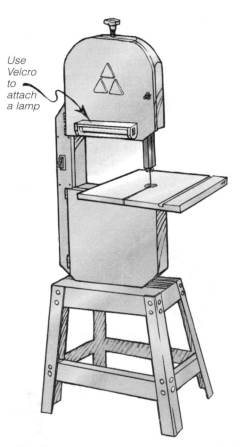

Use Velcro to attach a lamp

Quick Tip

Large assemblies with numerous parts can quickly get out of hand, so the pros know the value of a storyboard to keep everything organized. This can be as simple as a large sheet of paper or hardboard laid on the workbench, with a full-size template drawn on it. The template shows how the parts will be oriented to each other after assembly, and a good template can even be used to take measurements while you cut parts to size. Hot glue small guide blocks to the template, to help line up the larger parts.

Let There be Light

I equipped my band saw with a little 6" flourescent lamp that runs on AA batteries. I attached it with Velcro® and placed strips in other strategic spots around the shop. Now I have light wherever I need it.

Lawrence Heinonen
Burlington, Michigan

Q&A

"What's the difference between a dado, a rabbet and a groove?"

All three are rectangular grooves in wood. A dado runs across the grain, while a groove runs along the grain. A rabbet runs along the edge of a board.

Holder for a Drafting Lamp

Here's an idea that works on any workbench equipped with bench dog holes. Just take a piece of 2 x 4 and drill two holes several inches apart. One should fit the lamp base, while the other should be the same diameter as a bench dog.

Glue a dowel into the second hole and you can mount your lamp anywhere on the benchtop. The hinged arm on the lamp allows you to light up just about any project.

Harold A. Hubbard
Berkeley, California

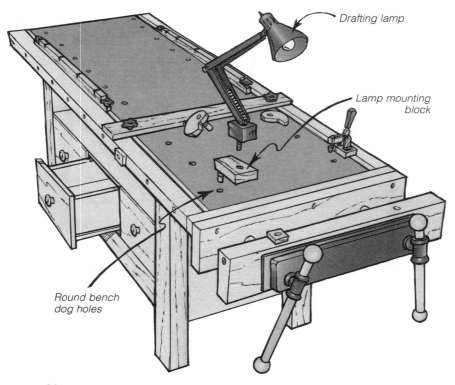

Drafting lamp

Lamp mounting block

Round bench dog holes

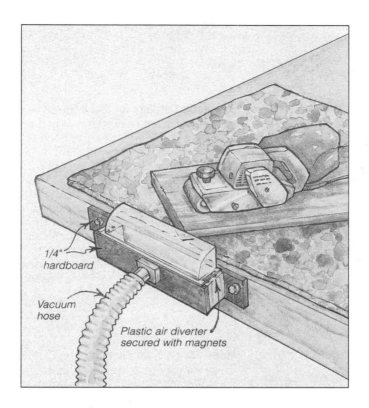

1/4" hardboard

Vacuum hose

Plastic air diverter secured with magnets

Inexpensive Dust Collection

I devised a dust catcher from a plastic register air diverter. These diverters come with magnets, so they can be mounted and removed in seconds. The hood attaches to a small box featuring a couple of 20d nails for the magnets to grab.

R. B. Himes
Vienna, Ohio

Legal-sized Tools

An old metal file cabinet makes a safe, dust-free storage device for power tools. And you can even organize them alphabetically!

Shay Thomas
Somerset, Wisconsin

Quick Tip

Those yellow, self-sticking notes that adorn every inch of the wall space in most office cubicles also come in a small size. It fits perfectly on the side of a 20-ft. tape measure — a real boon when you have several measurements to remember.

Q&A

"How can I make several identical small parts?"

The answer is template routing. Secure a 1/4" hardboard template to each blank in turn with two-sided tape, then use a bearing guided router bit (with the bearing on top) to cut the blank to shape. The bearing runs along the template. We suggest reading more about this technique before trying it, as it can be quite tricky.

Magnetic Catches for Small Boxes

Recently a friend asked me to make a box for his Irish flute. It needed to be free of outside projections, including hinges. Setting magnets into the box to secure the lid properly was my solution. I chopped three opposing mortises in the top and bottom edges of the box, and then epoxied the magnets in place. A strong and simple solution.

William Andersen
Chapel Hill, North Carolina

Keep Panels from Buckling

Here's a way to keep panels from buckling when they're edge-glued and clamped. I make custom end caps by plowing grooves in a couple of 2x4s the same dimension as the panel stock. So far, I haven't had a problem with the caps getting glued in place.

William P. Nichols
Ravenna, Ohio

2" x 4" with groove

2" x 4" with groove

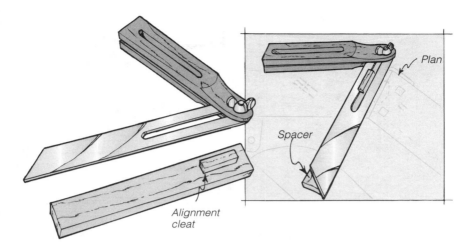

Plan

Spacer

Alignment
cleat

Sliding Jig for T-bevel

When I needed to transfer angles
from a plan to my workpiece,
I lost accuracy because the T-bevel
wouldn't lie flat. So I made a spacer
the same width as the bevel blade.
I added an alignment cleat that rides
in the blade slot.

Bob Kelland
St. John's, Newfoundland

Reduce Tearout

Remove finish nails from a board by
pulling them through with a pliers,
rather than hammering them back
out . You'll get less tearout.

Roger Berg
Farmington, Wisconsin

Raising More than a Panel

Stain raised panels before you install
them in their frames. Otherwise,
there will be an unstained line at the
edges if the panel shrinks.

John Tyler
Osceola, Wisconsin

Quick Tip

*Your local sawmill may be
a great source for
inexpensive lumber, but
moisture can be a problem.
Most small mills pile up logs
and store them out in the
weather. When they rip
them into boards, they
usually store these outside
in unprotected stickered
stacks. Bring a moisture
meter with you, and cross-
cut a board to test it: don't
test exposed ends. Accept
boards with 6% to 12%
moisture content.*

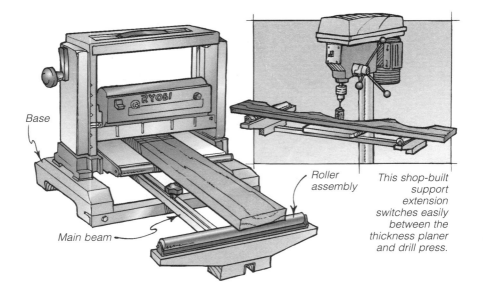

Base

Main beam

Roller assembly

This shop-built support extension switches easily between the thickness planer and drill press.

Q&A

"Is there an easy way to chop through mortises without a mortising machine or drill press attachment?"

Through mortises house a tenon that reaches all the way through the mortise and out the other side. They can often be made by cutting a shallow dado in each half of a leg (or other furniture part), then gluing the two halves together.

Make Your Own Support Extensions
The main component of this support system is a square tube attached to the drill press with two carriage bolts and T-knobs, or to the planer with two threaded T-knobs. The roller assemblies are always level and move vertically with the drill press table. The roller assembly is mounted on a support made of two pieces of 3/4" stock glued together, then mounted on the square tube. With the exception of the rollers, the entire system cost less than $10.
Raymond P.Cetnar
Amsterdam, New York

Here's a Good Point
Use a standard push pin from your bulletin board to transfer patterns from paper to wood. Just tape the pattern in place, then prick through it into the wood every 1/4" or so.
Charlotte Cole
Watertown, South Dakota

Plugging Holes in Premium Wood

To shave wood plugs absolutely flush, cut five pieces of paper to fit in the opening in your router base. Stack the paper and adjust a flat bit's height so it barely touches the top paper. Now run the router across the plug. If the bit still needs to come down, remove a couple of papers and repeat the adjustment until the plug is barely above the surface. Finish with a light sanding.

James A. Johnson
Brunswick, Ohio

Straight-up Chiseling

For chopping out waste in joinery, I use a chisel block to keep my chisel vertical. This is a hardwood block (about 2" thick) with a sandpaper bottom to keep it from moving. One bottom edge has a 1/4" chamfer, so my scribe line stays visible.

Nina Childs Johnson
(from a Woodworker's Journal article)

Quick Tip

You can significantly improve the quality of a rubbed glue joint (two boards joined on edge) by putting a pencil mark on the top of each board, then running them through the jointer. Keep one board's mark against the fence, and the other away from it. Then, if the jointer is even the tiniest bit out of alignment, the two cuts will compensate each other. Turn one board end-for-end, apply glue, and press them together: this will spread the glue more evenly. Then realign the boards correctly before clamping.

Q&A

"My air compressor just won't work on an extension cord. Any ideas?"

The manufacturer's instructions on most small compressors tell you to use a long air hose instead of an extension cord, because the latter can lower the amperage and damage the compressor's air pump.

Don't Wiggle your Joint

Never wiggle joints apart after a dry fit, as this will crush the wood fibers and cause a loose fit. Instead, use a mallet and a scrap block to tap the joint apart.

Nina Childs Johnson
(from a Woodworker's Journal article)

Miter Jig

My contractor's saw needed help to cut accurate miters, so I built this jig. Start with a keyed platform that rides in one miter gauge slot, and run it through the blade to trim it. Make an angled platform at 48° (no, that's not a misprint), then screw a fence to this at 90° to the blade. Tilt the blade until you have a perfect 45° angle, and remember to reset it to 90° when you're done.

Carl Allen
Oswego, New York

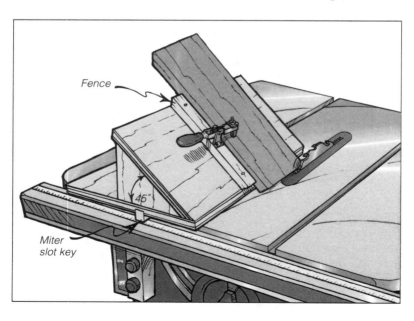

Fence

45°

Miter slot key

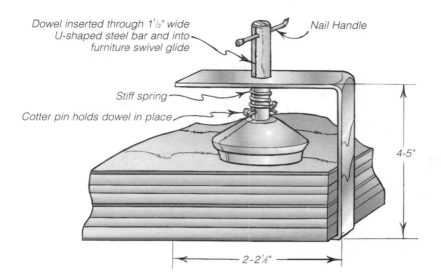

Dowel inserted through 1¹⁄₂" wide U-shaped steel bar and into furniture swivel glide

Nail Handle

Stiff spring

Cotter pin holds dowel in place

4-5"

2-2¹⁄₂"

Shop Built Clamps

It may be true that you can't have too many clamps, but they do get expensive! Using affordable items (springs, dowels, cotter pins and steel bars), I have crafted several versatile little clamps that work quite well for attaching trim and doing other light-duty jobs.

R. B. Himes
Vienna, Ohio

Magnify to Look Sharp

As you prepare to sharpen tools, set out the strop, stones, lubricant ... and a magnifying glass, loupe or optivisor! Being able to see and evaluate the cutting edge you are sharpening is as important as your technique. Often, what seems like a sharp edge will, under magnification, look more like a saw.

Michael Burton
Ogden, Utah

Quick Tip

As dust flies through your collector hoses, it builds up static electricity on the walls. To prevent sparks (and even explosions), you should ground metal hoses by attaching a piece of plastic-covered copper wire to the hose and a cold water pipe (or similar ground). Run bare wire through plastic hoses and ground one end of this in the same fashion.

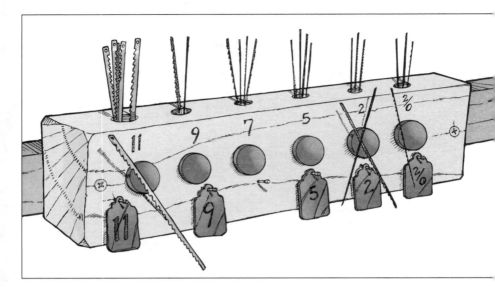

Q&A

"Can I use 3-phase stationary tools in my shop?"

3-phase current supplies a lot more amperage (power), so it's the norm in large commercial shops. Home shops generally don't have this option, but it's possible to buy a converter to step standard household current up to 3-phase.

Memory Magnets
I built this simple jig to organize my scroll saw blades. Whenever I install a blade, I attach the relevant number tag to the saw. When I get back to it a week or so later, I can immediately tell what number blade is installed. When I change blades, I stick the used one to the magnet in front of the correct hole, so it doesn't get mixed up with brand new blades.

Art Gustafson
Cobleskill, New York

Carpet Tape to the Rescue
If you run out of adhesive-backed sanding disks, you can make your own in a pinch with two-sided carpet tape and standard sandpaper. Trim along the edge of the metal disk with a utility knife before using it.

Edward Daniel, Jr.
Davenport, Iowa

Project Support

With a roller, a knob with threaded 3/8" stub, a 3/8" insert, some screws and scrap hardwood, I constructed a stand to support long projects being drilled on my benchtop drill press. The base of the support has a square opening about 1/16" larger than the support piece on either side, so the support will easily slide into the base. To provide for varying heights, a knob with a 1/8" threaded stub presses a moveable block against the support. I installed a threaded metal insert in the front block. To minimize wear, I epoxied a shoulder washer with a small hole to the moveable block. The top platform holds the roller while extending about 1/2" on each end.

Paul Feldker
Waterloo, Illinois

Quick Tip

Frame and panel doors don't just look pretty: they also perform a vital function. A free-floating panel is just about the only way to accommodate movement, especially when you're working in solid hardwoods. Resolving the movement issue is critical when the doors are inset: if they expand, you won't be able to open them until winter!

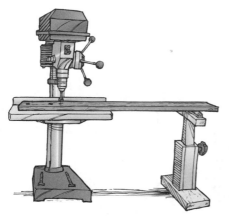

This benchtop jig supports long boards on the drill press

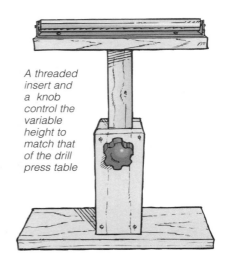

A threaded insert and a knob control the variable height to match that of the drill press table

Q&A

"Why use a veneered panel instead of edge-glued solid hardwood boards?"

A clear hardwood log yields thirty square feet of veneer to every board foot of lumber, so it's more economical. Plus, on an MDF or plywood core, veneer is dimensionally stable. Because of that, veneer panels can be used as structural elements like legs, doors and tabletops, and not just for decoration: they will carry a load without moving.

Safer Panel Raising

Raising panels with a router bit can be pretty scary, unless you use a vertical bit that is partially buried in the fence. With these, you'll get the best results when you remove no more stock than 3/32" per pass.

Howard Blanding
Somerset, Wisconsin

Spin for a Drill Bit

Here's a drill bit holder design that makes it easy to pick out any bit with a spin. I'm legally blind, but I can still see the numbers on the edge of the lazy Susan. So far, I have three different types of bits and each has its own color-coded lazy Susan, together with a drill gauge in the center to help me select the right bit every time.

Bernard C. Wiklund
Minneapolis, Minnesota

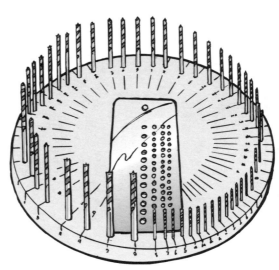

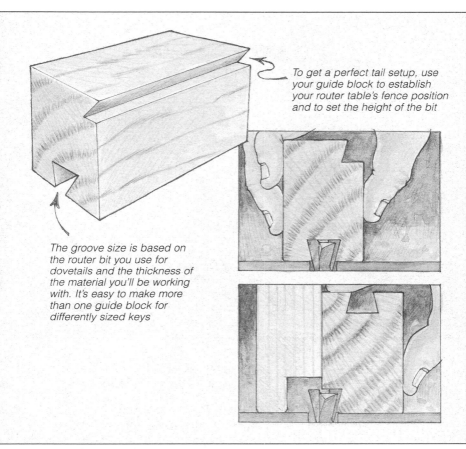

To get a perfect tail setup, use your guide block to establish your router table's fence position and to set the height of the bit

The groove size is based on the router bit you use for dovetails and the thickness of the material you'll be working with. It's easy to make more than one guide block for differently sized keys

The Key to Sliding Dovetails

Sliding dovetails make a great joint. There's a lot of gluing surface, they look great, and they hold forever. But they can be tricky to set up, unless you use a key. Making one is simplicity itself: just mill both the groove and the tail of a dovetail joint in the same hardwood scrap. Make one for each dovetail bit you own. Use a stable, tight-grained hardwood that won't expand or contract much, or even a piece of high density fiberboard. Now, instead of starting from scratch each time, you can just use the key to set the fence and the bit height.

R. B. Himes
Vienna, Ohio

Quick Tip

Between shop sessions, you can seal the top of your glue bottle with a sandwich bag (squeeze out the air first) and a rubber band. Use the band to store the bag on the side of the bottle during use.

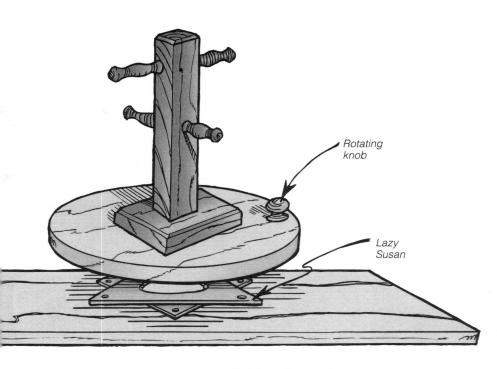

Rotating knob

Lazy Susan

Q&A

"I stained and lacquered my cabinet doors, but they're too light. What do I do?"

Mix some darker aniline dye into the lacquer, and apply another topcoat. Try it on some scrap first, then experiment on the backs of the doors, before applying it to the visible faces.

Finishing Carousel

An old retractable TV shelf with a lazy Susan makes an ideal finishing jig. Secure a 16" diameter plywood disk to the top, and you're ready to go to work.

Robert O. Wendel
Marlboro, New Jersey

Roll out the Paintbrush...

I often line the small boxes I make with felt. After spraying adhesive, I press the material onto the drawer bottom using what was once the handle of a "throwaway" paint brush. I cut it off just above the metal ferrule and then round over the edges to make a felt-friendly roller.

Ann Erlich
Long Beach, California

Twine Around your Laminate

Rather than fuss with dowels or shims when applying laminate, I use heavy twine (like the post office kind) to separate the two surfaces that have been coated with contact cement.

Frank Wyatt
Galax, Virginia

A Pin in the Hole Stops Slips

If the back saw in your manual miter box likes to jump out of the guide during the backstroke, pop a cotter pin in the hanging hole in the blade.

C. M. Wegner
Bloomington, Minnesota

Recycle a Circular Saw Base

When your circular saw gives out, save the base and recycle it as an adjustable guide for your drill press.

Ralph Wilkes
Penn Yan, New York

Quick Tip

To measure a museum piece, take a 35mm slide of it and measure one part (say, a 30" long leg). At home, you can adjust your projector and screen until the image of that leg is 30". Then all the other parts will be full scale.

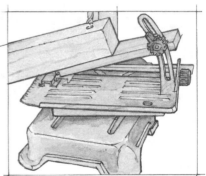

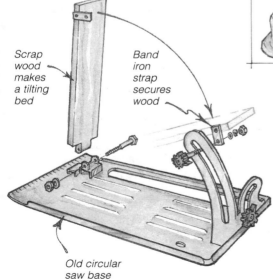

Scrap wood makes a tilting bed

Band iron strap secures wood

Old circular saw base

Notch the end of the scrap hardwood tilting bed to fit the hinge cradle on the old circular saw base, then drill a hole through the tongue you created, for a bolt.

Permanently tighten the bevel adjusting knob to keep the tilting bed in a horizontal position.

Q&A

"What is a quartersawn board?"

Imagine looking at the end of a large log. Now, think of cutting a 1x10 board out of that log, where one 1" edge of the board is at the center of the log, and the other is out near the bark. The wide (10") face of this board would have a long, tight, straight grain pattern with no crowns: this makes it very stable — it doesn't move much in humidity or temperature changes, so it's ideal for furniture building. A more common plain sawn board is cut at 90° to the quartersawn board (a much more economical way to mill), so it has crowns in its wide grain pattern.

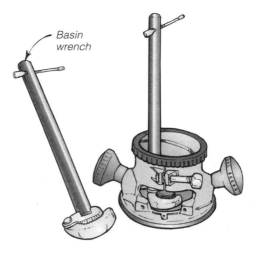

Basin wrench

Tightening Guide Nuts

When I have trouble tightening the locking nuts on my router guides, it's time to get out the basin wrench. I find it saves time, and wear and tear on my knuckles.

Jack Zabel
Cedar Falls, Iowa

Another Pitch for Baking Soda

Here is an environmentally responsible way to clean pitch from saw blades and router bits. In a plastic dishpan, with an inch of boiling water to cover the blade, I sprinkle a couple of tablespoons of baking soda around the perimeter of the blade. Within a minute the pitch is gone. I remove heavier deposits with a nail brush charged with baking soda, then dry with a hair dryer. Now, my bits and the environment are both a little cleaner.

Dennis DiVito
Buena Vista, Virginia

The Best Use for a Credit Card

I like to spread glue with an old credit card, after first trimming one end with a pair of pinking shears. The notches leave ribbons of glue that spread evenly when pressure is applied. This works wonderfully on large areas, such as when two boards are face-glued together.

Larry Heinonen
Burlington, Michigan

We Brake for Broken Screws!

We use a 5" length of 1/4" steel brake line in a drill to cut around finish nails and broken screws. A three-corner file is used to make pointed notches in one end of the tube, and these teeth cut down around the fastener. In a reversible drill, the tube sometimes reverses broken screws right out. Then we re-drill for a matching 3/8" wood plug and complete the repair.

Robert and Alice Tupper
Canton, South Dakota

Quick Tip

Resawing makes two thin boards (say, 5/16") out of one thick one (3/4"). It's usually done on the band saw with a stiff 1/2" or 5/8" blade. The best way to guide the board is to clamp a point fence to the saw. That's just a V-shaped fence, where the point is positioned the thickness of the resawn board (5/16") away from the blade. The idea is to keep the board vertical.

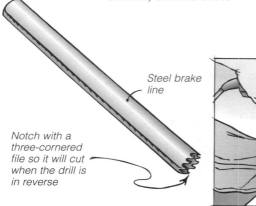

Steel brake line

Notch with a three-cornered file so it will cut when the drill is in reverse

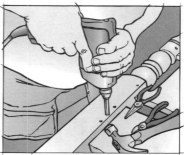

Q&A

"Is there any maintenance

I should be doing on my

air compressor?"

Yes. You should drain it after

every use (more frequently

on humid days with heavy

use), and you should place

one drop of oil in your nail

gun's coupler every time

you attach it to the air hose.

Keeping Pencils Handy

I keep a 1x2 slab of styrofoam near my drill press to store pencils close to my work. I just stab them into it. I also use the slab when working with screws, so they don't get lost.

George Suchy
Bradley, Illinois

PVC Collet Couples Vacuum Hose

The 2" dust port on my stationary sander didn't fit my ShopVac® hose. A short piece of schedule 40 PVC provided the solution. Several 2" saw kerfs turned one end into a collet that could securely grab the dust port. The other end was just the right size to fit the ShopVac hose.

J. David Carlson
Cary, North Carolina

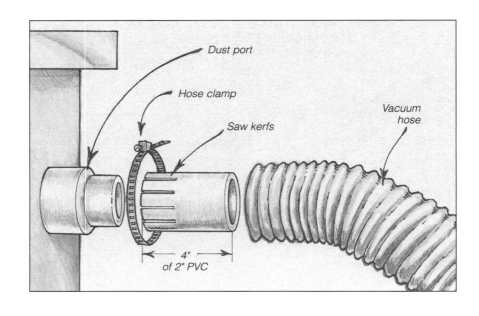

Dust port

Hose clamp

Saw kerfs

Vacuum hose

4"
of 2" PVC

Teflon Keeps Finish Fresh

While clear glass jars are handy for storing finishes, the caps often seal to the jar so opening them becomes both difficult and dangerous.

I found a simple solution: Teflon tape – the kind plumbers use. I wipe the top of the jar clean, then wrap a couple of layers of tape over the threads, going in the same direction the cap turns. I even let some tape lap over the top lip of the container. Most finishes and paints won't stick to the tape, so opening the jar becomes easy.

Teflon tape

Howard E. Moody
Upper Jay, New York

New Use for Old Putty Knife

I had a 2" putty knife with a stiff blade that I never used, so I applied 2-sided tape to the blade and stuck two different grades of sandpaper to it. Now I can clean up in tight spots.

Joe Cormier
Peabody, Massachusetts

Stable Straightedge

I made several stable straightedges by laminating strips of poplar and Philippine mahogany. I use them as winding sticks: the mix of dark and light woods shows up any problems.

Harold A. Hubbard
Berkeley, California

Quick Tip

Small, thin moldings can be quite hazardous when you try to mill them on a router, shaper or table saw. They are so light that the cutter can grab them and pull them out of your control in a split second, or shatter them and send pieces into orbit. The safest way to make a small molding is to mill it on the edge of a wide board, then just rip it to width on the table saw. Always keep the small cutoff on the side of the blade that's furthest from the fence, so it doesn't bind.

Q&A

"Why do the nails in my air gun keep blowing out the sides of my cabinets?"

Pneumatic nails are flat and two-sided, so they have a natural tendency to follow the grain. To prevent this, rotate the gun 90° so the nail head cuts across the grain. Another common cause of blow-out is driving nails that are simply too large for the application. You may want to try down-sizing, and see if that helps. You could also check the pressure you're using: it may be too high.

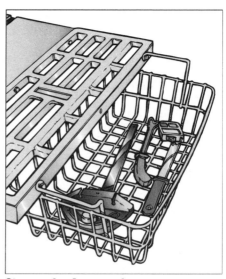

Storage for Accessories

If you fasten a metal mesh basket to the underside of your table saw, you'll have an excellent place to keep the miter gauge and push sticks — things that never seem to be handy when you need them. The mesh lets sawdust fall through, too.

Fred Boczek
DuBois, Illinois

Free CDs are a Big Hit

I used to be annoyed when those free Internet CDs arrived in the junk mail, but now I look forward to them. They make great shims for a wobbly workbench, trim protectors when you're painting a patch in the wall, glue spreaders, and a hundred other little shop helpers.

Roger Berg
Farmington, Wisconsin

Let Dyes Dissolve

Water-based aniline dyes have become increasingly popular in these environmentally-conscious days. These are colored powders that are dissolved in water, so large batches of stain can be made at very little expense. However, it's important to let the dye sit for an hour or two as some powders may take these that long to dissolve and yield their final color.

John Tancabel
St. Paul, Minnesota

Use this quick and simple depth gauge when you need to know the exact depth of a hole or mortise

Common 8d nail

Poor Man's Depth Gauge

You can save a few bucks and make a fairly accurate depth gauge with a nail and a wine bottle cork. Set the cork on the surface and run the nail down through it until its point hits the bottom of the hole you're measuring.

R. B. Himes
Vienna, Ohio

Quick Tip

Kiln-dried lumber can produce a lot of surprises if the operator doesn't know what he's doing. One of the most common defects, case-hardening, is the result of too rapid drying. The outside of each board dries quickly, causing the moisture in the center to be trapped. This moisture heats up, expands, and causes the wood to split (or "honeycomb") and virtually disintegrate. If you're buying a large load of freshly kilned lumber, ask the operator to rip one or two boards down their center, to check for case-hardening.

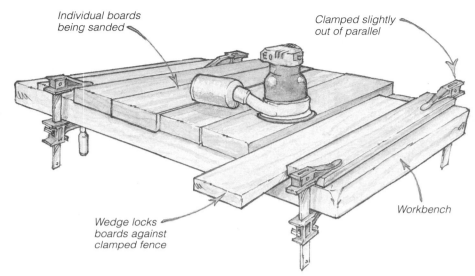

Individual boards being sanded

Clamped slightly out of parallel

Workbench

Wedge locks boards against clamped fence

Q&A

"How do I get a good glue bond with oily woods like teak?"

Start by rubbing the glue area with acetone (in a well vented area!) to get rid of any residual oils. After the acetone evaporates, you should double the clamping time for a surefire bond.

Sanding Jig for Multiple Boards

When I need to sand several boards of the same size, I clamp two fences to my bench, leaving one at a very slight angle to the other. Then I load up the boards and wedge them in place with a piece of scrap. It makes for very quick board changes, which is great on big jobs. Just make sure the fences and wedge are thinner than the boards being sanded.

Robert Jobsky
Goleta, California

Cleaning Sanding Belts and Disks

Spray oven cleaner on your gummed up belts and disks, then scrub them with a brass brush to loosen tars and resins. After they dry, use a regular rosin cleaner to finish the job and you'll have (almost) new abrasives.

Peter Przekop
Wilkes Barre, Pennsylvania

Hot Glue Helper

Keeping the corners square while you're cutting picture frame parts can be difficult, especially if the stock isn't rectangular. I apply just enough hot-melt glue on each corner to hold it temporarily, but not so much that I can't break the joint to make adjustments before a final glue-up with yellow glue.

Ben Crowe
Blackshear, Georgia

Quick Tip

It is absolutely vital to take certain precautions when spraying finishes. Use a NIOSH approved Organic Vapor N95 respirator (95% efficient): standard dust masks offer no protection from airborne finishes. Work in a properly ventilated area, as higher concentrations of many chemicals have been linked to cancer, nerve damage and respiratory diseases. Wear eye protection, and always know where your co-workers are: even HVLP-driven low pressure sprays can penetrate skin.

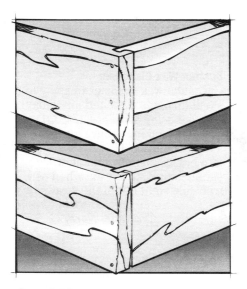

Growth Ring Joinery

For tight box or drawer corners, arrange the parts so that all the annual growth rings curve out toward the ends. Wood tends to cup in the direction opposite to the rings' curve, so if you crown the board the wrong way the rings may draw the joinery apart.

Joe Nelson
S. CelElum, Washington

After the wax cools, slip it out of the straw and into an eraser holder

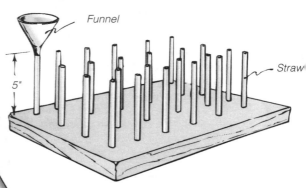

Funnel

5"

Straw

Q&A

"How efficient are HVLP sprayers, as compared to regular ones?"

A standard, inexpensive high pressure gun for your air compressor will deliver about 25% of the finish to the workpiece. HVLP (high volume low pressure) spray systems deliver between 65% and 90%, depending on the product.

Custom Wax Dispenser

Carnauba wax is easier to apply to small turnings if melted into small sticks using standard 1/4" OD plastic drinking straws for forms. The resulting 7/32" stick fits handily into eraser holders sold at office supply stores. The wax, when set, will slide right out of the straws.

Bill Skinner
Charlotte, North Carolina

How to Erase Burns

To eradicate router or saw burns, brush on a solvent (naptha, alcohol, mineral spirits — even water), let it soak for a minute, then sand. Mineral spirits works best, and my Dremel tool is ideal for the sanding stage. Here, diamond burrs are my tool of choice, but sandpaper can also be used.

Stan Kasieta
Woodline, Michigan

Quick Allen Action

I like to cut the "L" off some of my spare Allen wrenches and leave a straight end that can be chucked in a drill. It's a great timesaver when assembling knock-down furniture.

Roger Berg
Farmington, Wisconsin

Flush your Dust!

A commode floor flange is a perfect fit for a 4" dust collector hose. I screwed one to a piece of 3/4" plywood and hooked up my contractor's saw to the dust collection system. Cost was about $5.

Rex Roach
Opelika, Alabama

Quick Tip

There's nothing quite as elegant as clear strapping tape when it comes to clamping unusual shapes. A good quality tape can be stretched to its limits and, as its memory makes it try to shrink back to its original size, it draws parts together for a perfect bond.

Mitered corners are especially suited to this technique. First, apply a short strip of tape to create a hinge, then spread the glue and close the miter. Finally, stretch the tape across it to draw it tight.

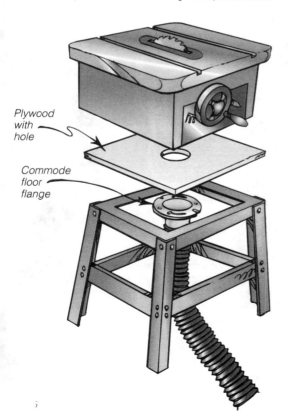

Plywood with hole

Commode floor flange

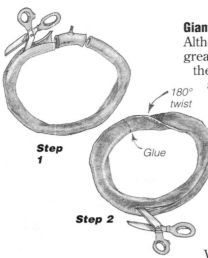

Step 1

180° twist

Glue

Step 2

Giant Band Clamps

Although bicycle inner tubes make great band clamps, sometimes even they are not big enough. Here's a science class trick that will double their size. Cut out a couple of inches to remove the valve, then split the remainder lengthways. Now bring the ends together, and twist one a half turn (180°). Apply 2" of tire patching cement to join them and, after it dries, make another cut and slice all the way around the circumference. When the cut returns to the starting point, you'll have one big rubber band, not two small ones, thanks to the twist you put in earlier.

R. B. Himes
Vienna, Ohio

Q&A

"How do I make stable butcherblock out of ordinary plain sawn boards?"

Rip a plain sawn board into strips that are 1/16" thicker than the new counter or tabletop you're making, then turn these 90° before jointing their edges and re-gluing them together. This will give you a stable, quartersawn panel.

Step 3

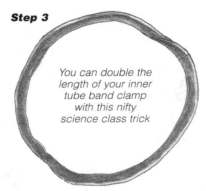

You can double the length of your inner tube band clamp with this nifty science class trick

Raising Grain

To repair a minor indent in unfinished stock, place a few drops of water in the indent, then heat it up with a clothes iron to raise the grain. Finish up by sanding it smooth.

John Tyler
Osceola, Wisconsin

Shaving-free Lathe Tool Caddy

I wanted my woodturning lathe tools to be sharp, near and clean. So I built a simple caddy to hold them. It hugs the lathe bed securely with a dozen ring magnets embedded in its underside. I just slide this caddy close to my work, and the tools remain clean as the chips fall through the wire mesh bottom.

Dick Dorn
Oelwein, Iowa

Getting the Point

Finishing cabinet doors can be a real time chewer, because you generally have to wait for the first side to dry before you can tackle the second. I drove 8d finish nails through some 2" square blocks of 1x pine, then set them on the bench with the points facing up. Then I placed the doors face down on the points of the nails, finished the backs (which were facing up), and then immediately turned them over and finished the fronts and edges.

Shay Thomas
Somerset, Wisconsin

Quick Tip

The moisture content of wood is measured in terms of weight: the weight of the water versus the weight of the wood. On average, the ideal moisture level in stock about to be milled is around 7%: that is, the moisture in the wood should weigh 7% of what the wood weighs. Freshly cut green wood can have a moisture level as high as 200%. In that case, the moisture weighs twice what the wood alone weighs. Cross-cut a board to measure the moisture, as the ends and outer surfaces will be drier than the core.

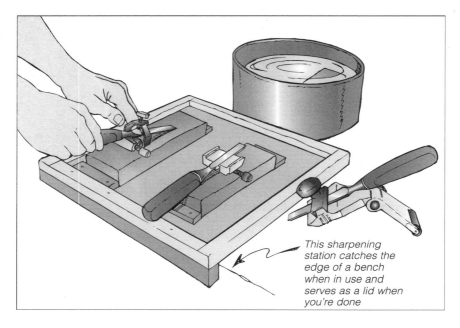

This sharpening station catches the edge of a bench when in use and serves as a lid when you're done

Q&A

"Why is Spanish cedar used in cigar humidors?"

This species is rich in aromatic oils that enhance the flavor of cigar smoke. It is also easy to work, attractive and decay-resistant (which is an asset in a humid container).

Sharpening Station

You'll be more likely to sharpen chisels and plane irons when they need it if you have a sharpening station. Begin by cutting 6" off the bottom of a 5-gallon bucket and use this to keep your stones immersed in water or oil. Cut a 20" square plywood base and rout a circular groove in the bottom to turn it into a lid for the bucket. Nail strips of wood around the top so water or oil won't escape while you work. Nail a small strip at either end of each stone to hold them when they're not immersed, and a final strip under the front edge to catch the edge of your bench: this will hold the station steady as you sharpen because the lid won't slip when you push on the stones.

Jeff Greef
Soquel, California

Chuck Key Keeper

Drill a hole in your drill press chuck key and use a split key ring to thread it onto the power cord: now it will always be close to the tool.

Noel Griffith
Monroe, New York

Mitered Moldings

Moldings that have a repeating pattern on them need to be addressed at the design stage. The plan must be adjusted so the pattern matches up perfectly at the corners. One way to do this is to create a full-size drawing of the parts and test the molding's pattern on it. If resizing won't work, switch moldings.

Rick White
Medina, Minnesota

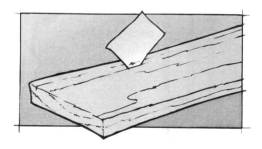

Evaluating Surface Checks

Some surface checks (short cracks) will come off in planing, while others go into the heart of the board. To see how deep they are, I simply insert the corner of a piece of paper.

Michael Burton
Glorieta, New Mexico

Quick Tip

Pine drawers have traditionally had hardwood runners, so the grooves in the pine drawer sides tend to wear out first. You can avoid this in new construction by milling a wide groove along the outside face of each drawer side, then gluing in a hardwood strip. After the glue dries, sand the strip flush, then mill a smaller groove in the hardwood insert for the drawer runner to ride in. This is also a great retrofit for an older, existing cabinet that has sloppy action in its pine drawers. Wax the slots with candle wax.

Q&A

"I want to assemble

a cabinet with screws and

dadoes, but my screws

always seem to just miss

the center of the dado. Any

ideas?"

Instead of assembling the

carcass, and then trying to

locate the screws from the

outside by measuring, just

drill pilot holes out from the

inside before assembly.

That way, you can set the

bit right in the middle of the

dado each time. And with

the pilot holes established,

you can now countersink

where the drill bit exited.

Never, Ever Let Go!

No matter how rough things get, or how probable a kickback will be, don't ever let go of the wood while your table saw blade is still spinning. You're not fast enough to get out of the way of a 50 MPH projectile. More often than not, by holding on, you will actually prevent kickback. Over the years I've trained my reflexes not to panic and jump away, so now I hold on tighter than ever. I even drive the piece forward if I can, depending on the circumstances.

Rick Christopherson
Eagan, Minnesota

A Dolly Extension

When I hauled trash cans and other large loads on my two-wheel dolly, they tended to tip. So I designed a small platform that enlarges the base of the dolly, providing a more stable and roomy platform. The 1/4" spacer strips are just thick enough to accommodate the dolly's blade freely.

Ron Pavelka
Orange, California

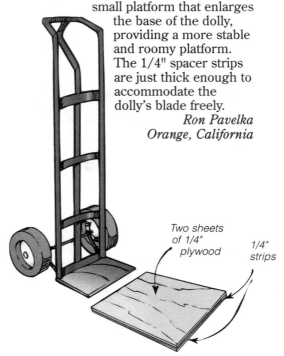

Two sheets
of 1/4"
plywood

1/4"
strips

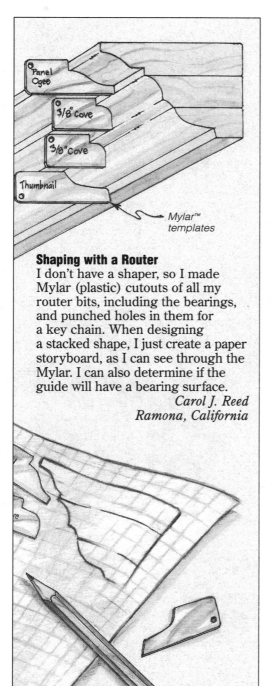

Mylar™ templates

Shaping with a Router

I don't have a shaper, so I made Mylar (plastic) cutouts of all my router bits, including the bearings, and punched holes in them for a key chain. When designing a stacked shape, I just create a paper storyboard, as I can see through the Mylar. I can also determine if the guide will have a bearing surface.

Carol J. Reed
Ramona, California

Quick Tip

The specialty bit used to create two-stage holes for pocket screws is basically a 3/8" bit with a 1/8" pilot bit stuck into its business end. If you own one, you know just how susceptible to damage they are.

Gerald Wallin of St. Paul, Minnesota, suggests protecting the delicate pilot bit by using it to bore a 2" deep hole into a scrap block. You can then store the bit right in the scrap block. The friction fit turns the block into a nice, protective storage cap.

Q&A

"What causes kickback on my table saw?"

Kickback is caused by one or both of the following: an underpowered saw, and incorrect blade height. If your saw is heavy and powerful enough, it will keep cutting through a twist, bind or improperly fed piece of stock. If your blade is set too low, the teeth are meeting the wood horizontally instead of vertically: in the latter case, they would force the wood down on the table, but in the former they are pushing the stock right at you.

Solving the Tan Foam Problem

The new polyurethane glues leave a tan foam around the glue line and stain on your hands. I take a rag dampened with lacquer thinner and wipe the glue line when it is foamed but still sticky. Take care not to get the solvent in the joint, where it will dissolve the glue. For my hands, I keep a jar of dishwashing soap and lacquer thinner, about an inch of each, in the shop.

Dave Palmer
Royal Oak, Michigan

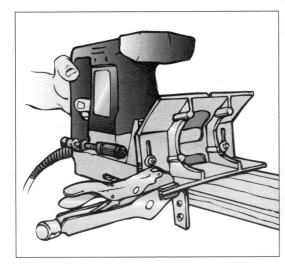

Stopping Biscuit Joiner Drift

The alignment pins on my biscuit joiner are too far apart to center a slot in the end of a narrow board. So, where a job requires numerous slots in the same position, I use vise grips and a small angle bracket to position the joiner where I need it.

Tommy Capps
Plano, Texas

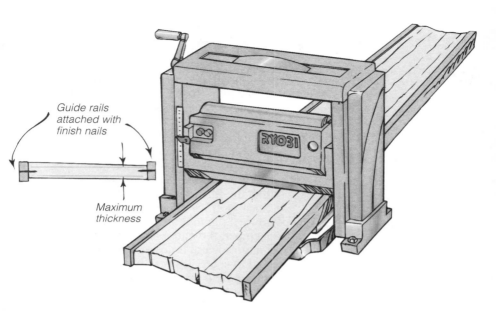

Guide rails attached with finish nails

Maximum thickness

Straightening Twisted Lumber

Rough lumber with a diagonal twist can be difficult to straighten, unless you use this trick. Joint the edges of the board and set it on a flat surface. Shim the two high corners, then rip two guide rails from scrap stock: their height should be the same as the highest spot on the shimmed board, and they should be cut from straight hardwood. Finish nail these in place, keeping the nails as close to the center of the guide rails as possible, so they never come in contact with the planer knives. Then run the assembly through the planer (or a wide belt sander equipped with a coarse grit belt), alternating the sides: the top should be up on the first pass, down on the second, and so on, until the board is flat. The guide rails will keep the board perfectly aligned.

William Woodward
Hunlock Creek, Pennsylvania

Quick Tip

The best finish for children's toys and furniture may well be shellac, because it becomes totally nontoxic once it's dry. Shellac has even been approved by the FDA for certain applications, including drug and candy coatings.

Q&A

"Why do the pros laminate or veneer both sides of a countertop?"

They do this to keep the assembly as stable as possible, so that it will stay as flat as possible. If the top face alone were laminated, ambient humidity might enter the porous face on the underside, and that inequality is an invitation to warping. Some of the core products the pros use in cabinet shops even come from the factory with a plastic coating already applied to the underside, so the shop doesn't have to spend time laminating the underside.

Shelf Solution

When using screws or nails to attach fixed shelves in a cabinet carcass, I use a neat trick that lets me line up my shelves perfectly every time. Using a square, I draw a pencil line across each of the cabinet's sides at the center (half the thickness) of each shelf. Next, I drill holes through the sides slightly smaller than my nails will be, then set my marking gauge for half the thickness of the shelves. Starting from the ends, I work toward the middle (to avoid causing a chip at the ends) and draw the gauge several times across each end to score it. With the carcass assembled, I tap nails through the sides so the tips protrude just 1/32". Then I hold the shelves up to the sides and feel the nail points fall into the grooves. As each nail finds its groove, I drive it home and set it.

James A. Johnson
Brunswick, Ohio

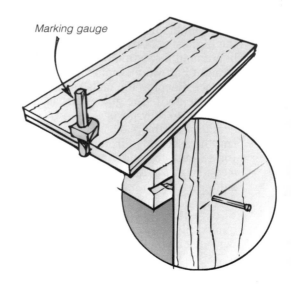

Marking gauge

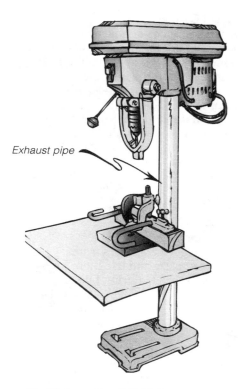

Exhaust pipe

Quick Tip

You can't mill a bullnose on the edge of a board with a bearing guided bit, at least not if you just rely on the bearing. After making the first cut, you've removed most of the bearing surface for the second cut, so it will be offset (the bit will remove more stock on the second cut than the first). The answer is to make both cuts using the same bearing-guided bit, but you have to rely on your router table's fence, instead of the bearing, to guide the cuts.

Modifying a Small Drill Press

My benchtop drill press was too short for any of the available mortising jigs. So I went to an auto parts store and, for $6, replaced the post on my press with a straight length of exhaust pipe.

Robert Opekun
Orange, Connecticut

Making Milk Paint

To make one gallon of traditional interior milk paint, mix 8 lbs. of skim milk, 8 oz. of linseed oil, 12 oz. slaked (garden) lime, and 6 lbs. of calcium carbonate (whiting).

Larry Fiscus
White Bear Lake, Minnesota

Q&A

"How do I apply a water-based aniline dye?"

After sanding the project to 120 grit, raise the grain with a damp sponge and sand with 220 grit paper. Add a drop of dish soap to the dye solution to help break the surface adhesion and let it penetrate properly. Apply the dye with a foam brush and wipe it off immediately with paper towels. Wear rubber gloves, as sweat can leave marks on the stain.

Budget Bushings

When a number of holes have to be drilled, a jig with a drill bushing comes in very handy. If you're ever caught without the bushing, try grabbing an appropriately sized T-nut instead. I install one in the jig and drill it out for the correct size drill. This trick won't hold up in daily use, but it sure works well for ten or twenty holes.

Jack Zabel
Cedar Falls, Iowa

Pizza Pedestals

Save the plastic spacers from delivered pizza and use them to support projects during finishing.

Randy Wells
Bethalto, Illinois

Stretch your Pipe Clamps

On those few occasions when you need an extra-long clamp, don't buy long pipes that will spend the rest of their lives in a dark corner. Just invest in a couple of pipe couplings and join two or more of your existing short lengths together.

Michael Burton
Ogden, Utah

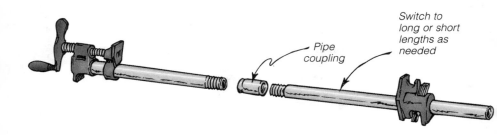

Pipe coupling

Switch to long or short lengths as needed

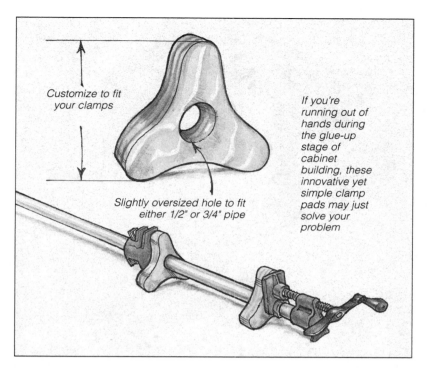

Customize to fit your clamps

If you're running out of hands during the glue-up stage of cabinet building, these innovative yet simple clamp pads may just solve your problem

Slightly oversized hole to fit either 1/2" or 3/4" pipe

Innovative Clamp Pads

Positioning a pad between the jaw of a bar clamp and the assembly you're building can be tricky. Trying to keep the clamps in position — especially when you're at the other end of a large cabinet — can be downright frustrating. My three-spoke pads solve both problems at once. Two of the three spokes become the stand's legs (they even allow for uneven surfaces), while the third spoke automatically centers itself as a hands-free pad between the metal of the clamp jaw and the workpiece being glued up.

R. B. Himes
Vienna, Ohio

Quick Tip

For worktops on outdoor projects like grills, tables and barbecue carts, some solid surface materials like Corian® work extremely well. You can pick up a sink cutout at a cabinet shop for a minor charge, or even for free. Although some products aren't certified for outdoor use, they all seem to hold up very well.

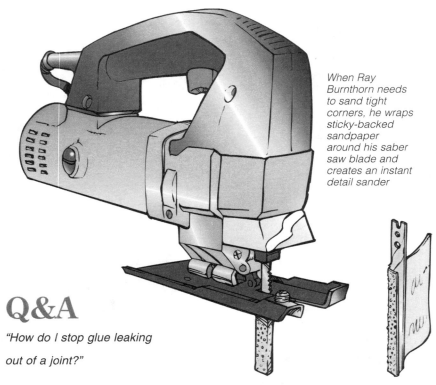

When Ray Burnthorn needs to sand tight corners, he wraps sticky-backed sandpaper around his saber saw blade and creates an instant detail sander

Q&A

"How do I stop glue leaking out of a joint?"

The easiest way to control glue is to use a sharp utility knife or a rotary cutter in a multi-tool (like a Dremel®) to score a small V-shaped channel just out of sight on the hidden parts of the joint. The groove should be about 1/8" in from the edge. Glue traveling toward the edge should settle in this groove.

Jigsander
Here's a terrific trick that I use when I make lawn ornaments. To clean up the intricate cuts, I wrap a piece of self-adhesive sandpaper around the jigsaw blade. You'll have to open the cooling blocks for this to work, and the stiffest blade I've found is a Porter Cable 12361.

Ray Burnthorn
Manteca, California

Sticky Sticks
If you're using plastic packing tape as a clamp, place a popsicle stick on either side of the glue joint to raise the tape out of the glue.

John Tancabel
St. Paul, Minnesota

Thinning your Aging Glue

Most yellow aliphatic resin glues (like the Titebond® brand that my employer makes) have a shelf life of about two years, and weatherproof glues can often last twice that long. If you're not sure how long your glue has been on the shelf, there's a quick way to test its usability. If it rolls up in a little ball or is rubbery, it's time to go shopping. Yellow glue should survive at least five freeze/thaw cycles: it will work just as well, but its consistency may change. Thick glue can be stirred, or you can even add up to 5% water without affecting the bonding strength.

Dale Zimmerman
Columbus, Ohio

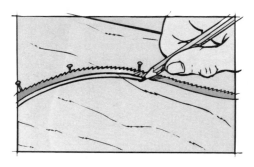

Drawing a Smooth Curve

An old band saw blade works wonderfully for drawing smooth curves. Drive nails at key spots along the waste side to guide it along.

Michael Burton
Ogden, Utah

Quick Tip

Because solid surface materials like Corian® are really just plastic, they can generally be worked with woodworking tools.

They do, however, require that you equip your tools with carbide blades and bits as they are usually about three times as dense as most hardwoods. Take your time: when routing a decorative edge, make several passes. To achieve a matte finish, start with 180 grit and work down to 400 grit, then buff with a green Scotchbrite® pad.

Q&A

"How do I make dentil molding?"

Dentil molding is a classic piece of trim that looks like a series of teeth and gaps (hence the name). The easiest way to mill it is to clamp a straightedge across a board and rout a dado, then screw a guide that has the same dimensions as the dado to the bottom of your router (you may want to attach a plywood base first). Then you can just run the guide in the groove you cut to mill the next groove, and so on. After all the grooves (or gaps) are cut, rip the board into strips that are whatever width you want your molding to be.

Large Cabinet, Small Shop

Your cabinet is all assembled and you're doing the final sanding. So, how do you protect the just-finished side when you lay it down to sand the opposite side? I prefer to use ceiling tiles — the type that don't have a hard surface — and place them on the floor or the bench.

Tom Palubecki
Milwaukee, Wisconsin

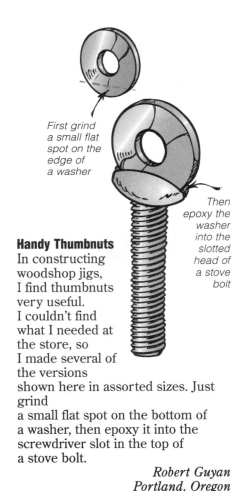

First grind a small flat spot on the edge of a washer

Then epoxy the washer into the slotted head of a stove bolt

Handy Thumbnuts

In constructing woodshop jigs, I find thumbnuts very useful. I couldn't find what I needed at the store, so I made several of the versions shown here in assorted sizes. Just grind a small flat spot on the bottom of a washer, then epoxy it into the screwdriver slot in the top of a stove bolt.

Robert Guyan
Portland, Oregon

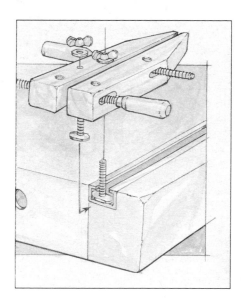

Quick Tip

Shellac flakes are mixed with denatured alcohol in various ratios, or cuts. One pound of shellac mixed with one gallon of alcohol produces what is called a "one-pound cut." A three-pound cut would still only have one gallon of alcohol, but three pounds of flakes. The lower the cut, the thinner the mix. That means more coats, but a smoother application. It's all a matter of personal preference. Either way, make sure you buy fresh flakes, as older stock will give you some serious application headaches.

Instant Workbench Vise

Most workbenches have two vises that allow you to work at either one side or an end. Mine only had one vise at the end, so I decided to use an embedded T-track on the bench to hold a couple of 10" screw clamps. All I had to do was drill a hole in each clamp and insert a T-bolt. A wingnut makes adjusting easy. Sliding one clamp in from each end gives me an instant vise.

Joe Cormier
Peabody, Massachusetts

Clean Magnets

When picking up iron or steel filings with a magnet, wrap the magnet in a paper cloth and you'll be able to discard the refuse more easily.

Harold Keenan
Danbury, Connecticut

Q&A

"How do I stop my large square from slipping when I use it as a straightedge to draw layout lines?"

This is a common problem, and the best solution we've seen is compliments of Michael Burton of Glorieta, New Mexico. Michael drilled several holes in his square, each the exact size of a metal push pin's shank (the kind you find on bulletin boards). The sharp point leaves such a small hole that it simply isn't an issue. Another suggestion is to apply a roll of 220 grit self-adhesive sandpaper to the bottom of the square.

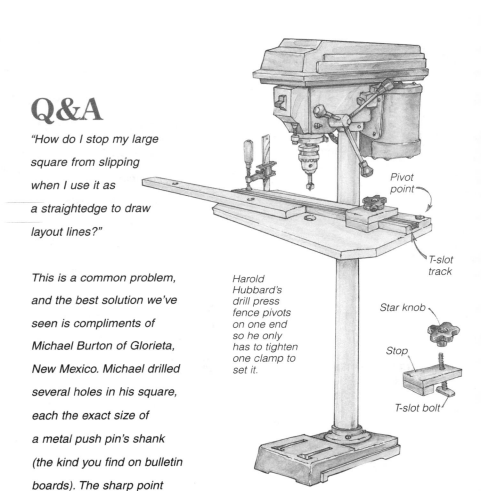

Harold Hubbard's drill press fence pivots on one end so he only has to tighten one clamp to set it.

T-slot for Instant Stops

I use a pivot fence on my drill press as it's easier to adjust than the ones that rely on C-clamps. For stops, I used T-slot hardware: bolt heads ride in the track which is incorporated in the fence, and my stops attach to the bolts via star knobs. They are infinitely adjustable and easily removed.

Harold A. Hubbard
Berkeley, California

Humidity Stick

I build and repair fine furniture for a living, and tracking humidity levels in my shop is critical to my success. A few years ago, I edge-glued several short lengths of 1" x 2" red oak together, then attached a strip of 3/4" x 2" hard maple to one end of the block. Ever since then, once a week I mark the other end's location on the maple and date it. I now have a track record of the humidity in my shop that tells me what times of the year the highs and lows occur, and an instant reference that can be checked on any given day.

Tom Caspar
Minneapolis, Minnesota

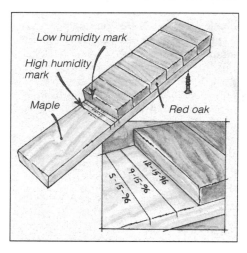

Low humidity mark

High humidity mark

Maple

Red oak

12-15-96
9-15-96
5-15-96

Substitute Work Supports

I was cutting a sheet of plywood and needed extra support when I noticed the family ironing board hanging in the corner. I figured, why not? It's smooth, inexpensive and everyone owns one. I got a great laugh from a fellow woodworker when I told him.

Joseph Roberge
Brown Mills, New Jersey

Quick Tip

When you're designing the joints in a piece of furniture or casework, think not only how they will look and work, but also how they will be machined. For example, if you install a 3/8" dado head in the table saw and set the height at 3/8", you can cut both parts of a rabbet and dado joint without ever changing your setup. If you place 3/8" dowel joints and 3/8" shelf supports in the same relative locations in a cabinet, you can use a single drill press setup for both tasks. And if you make stiles, rails and trim pieces the same width, you can rip and joint them all at the same time.

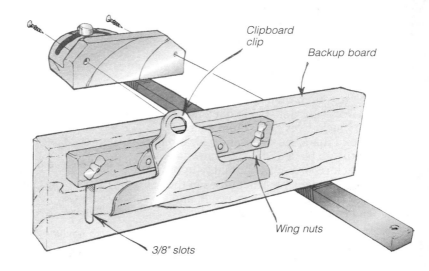

Clipboard clip

Backup board

Wing nuts

3/8" slots

Q&A

"Should I buy carbide-tipped or just high speed steel (HSS) router bits?"

The experts disagree on this issue. While most automatically answer carbide because it outlasts steel by 15 to 25 times, some pros like steel because they're a lot less expensive, they can be sharpened in the shop, and they can be ground to alter their shapes.

Small Stock Miter Gauge Clamp

Trying to hold small pieces of stock against a miter gauge can be tricky, but the stout spring and wide jaws of a clipboard clip can help. Attach the clip to a piece of scrap, which in turn is screwed to the miter gauge. You can also rout grooves in the scrap and use wing nuts to attach the clip: this lets you raise or lower the unit as needed. A scrap backup block reduces tearout.

R. B. Himes
Vienna, Ohio

Veneer Quick Dry

If you moisten veneer with water and glycerin to flatten it, here's a great way to dry it. Simply place it between sheets of corrugated packing material. The corrugations permit air movement and the sheet and material will withstand a terrific amount of weight. A fan can be used to speed drying.

Michael Burton
Ogden, Utah

Drum Sander Jig

When using a drum sander in the drill press, the sandpaper at the bottom always wears out first. To remedy this, I made a sanding box out of 3/4" particleboard that I clamp to the drill press table. Cut a $3^1/_2$" diameter hole in the top of the box for a 3" drum, and a $1^1/_2$" hole in the bottom for a 1" drum. Make the sides tall enough to fit the drums. You can now raise the table or lower the chuck to use all the sanding surface.

Martha Dawson
Squaw Valley, California

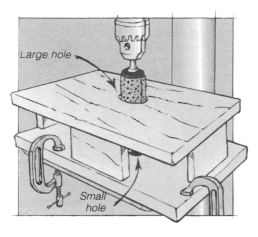

Large hole

Small hole

Getting Out the Glue

I always keep a couple of bottles of wood glue handy in my shop, but when I don't use them regularly, the tips get clogged. Now I use a 2-quart milk container with the top cut off to keep some water handy. Whenever I use a glue bottle, I replace the cap with a fresh one and submerge the used cap in the water.

Howard E. Moody
Upper Jay, New York

Quick Tip

If, like most of us, your budget will only allow you to buy either a shaper or a large router, the experts all say to go the latter route. Routers are more versatile and less expensive, plus they can do a lot of things a shaper can't — like mortising and using a dovetail jig. A shaper is definitely the right tool in large production jobs, but a big router can do pretty much everything a shaper can, only slower. While an industrial shaper with a $1^1/_4$" spindle can easily handle 4" stock in one pass, even a 3HP router will need to make several passes to do the same job.

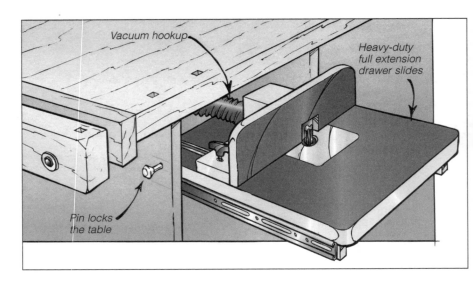

Vacuum hookup

Heavy-duty
full extension
drawer slides

Pin locks
the table

Q&A

"Do I have to throw away

my paint brushes when they

get stiff?"

Absolutely not. One of the

best ways to restore

brushes when the finish has

hardened is to soak them in

stripper for a few minutes.

Work the stripper up along

the bristles until all the

finish is loosened. Then

thoroughly wash the brush,

because stripper will loosen

the bristles if it's left alone.

Pull-out Router Table

In a small shop, my router table may create a little room. I used full extension, heavy-duty slides and added a locking pin to keep the table from moving during operation. When not in use, it slips right out of sight.

Thomas Pratley
Oxnard, California

Finger Protectors

When I sand small items, I protect my fingers with those flexible rubber tips that office supply stores sell to people who count money. They're cheap (about $2 a dozen), and they give you a good grip on small workpieces.

R. B. Himes
Vienna, Ohio

Inexpensive Quartersawn Stock

Need a small piece of quartersawn stock? Plain sawn boards all have quartersawn grain along their edges!

John Tancabel
St. Paul, Minnesota

Clay is handy in the Shop

I often need to paint small items of hardware (nail heads, screw eyes etc.) for use on one of my woodworking projects. I have found that a 1 lb. box of modeling clay is very handy for these jobs. The clay won't harden, yet is firm enough to hold assorted small parts for painting. It also works well for glue-ups.

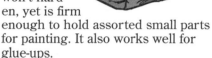

Howard Moody
Upper Jay, New York

Vibration Dampers

The heels from a tired pair of running sneakers generally have enough rubber-type material to make excellent vibration dampers for shop tools and tables. They can be custom cut with a bread knife. Use a Forstner bit to recess a bolt head and washer for mounting.

Joseph Fetchko
Ocean City, Maryland

Quick Tip

Certain wood species are naturally more resistant to exposure than others, so using one of them in outdoor projects is the way to go. Certified farm-raised teak is perhaps the most resilient, but it tends to be oily and often doesn't glue very well. White oak (not the common red variety) is far less expensive and does well outdoors, as do cedar, redwood, Spanish cedar and Honduras mahogany. The key is in the finish you apply: research is advised.

Q&A

"How do I get rid of snipe?"

Snipe is that annoying little concave area that a jointer or thickness planer leaves on the last couple of inches of a board. It is caused by an outfeed table that is set lower than the knives, or else the workpiece is just too short. Dealing with it involves adjusting the outfeed table, planing longer boards, or buying one of a new breed of planers that are marketed as being "snipe-free." Traditionally, woodworkers have just run boards that are 6" or 8" too long, then they've trimmed the snipe from the ends on the miter saw. It's not thrifty, but it works.

Hinged Board Jacks

Board jacks are used to support long boards clamped in a bench vise. I cut two 12" long pieces of 5/4 oak and attached one to each front leg of my workbench with a pair of butt hinges. I used a straightedge to keep the jacks at the same level as the bench vise. The hinges allow me to swing the jacks out of the way, alongside the legs but tucked under the overhangs at the ends of the bench, when I don't need them.

Kevin Hemmingsen
Wabasha, Minnesota

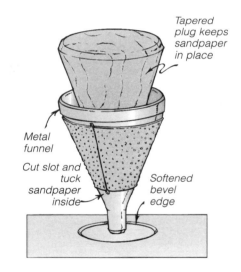

Tapered plug keeps sandpaper in place

Metal funnel

Cut slot and tuck sandpaper inside

Softened bevel edge

Hole Beveling Sanding Block

Putting a beveled edge on a hole is easy with a metal funnel. Cut a slit in the side, then wrap a sheet of sandpaper around the funnel with an inch or so of each end inside the slot. A tapered plug secures it.

R. B. Himes
Vienna, Ohio

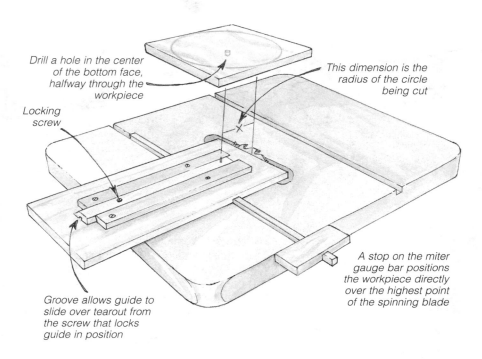

Drill a hole in the center of the bottom face, halfway through the workpiece

This dimension is the radius of the circle being cut

Locking screw

A stop on the miter gauge bar positions the workpiece directly over the highest point of the spinning blade

Groove allows guide to slide over tearout from the screw that locks guide in position

Cut Circles on the Table Saw

The base of this jig is just a platform with a bar that runs in the miter gauge slot. A guide slides across the top, locking into position with the turn of a screw to allow you to cut any radius. One end of the guide houses an upturned nail. To use the jig, drill a small pilot hole halfway through the center of the workpiece. Set the radius (the distance between the center of the pivot and the near edge of the blade), then drop the piece upside down on the nail. SLOWLY raise the blade 1/16" per full revolution of the workpiece. Rotate the piece slowly, too, or the wood will burn and may become airborne. For circles under 12", use a push stick. Always keep downward pressure on the wood above the nail.

Michael Trotter
Giebelstadt, Germany

Quick Tip

You can tell if the infeed and outfeed tables of a jointer are parallel by running some test boards and holding the jointed edges together. If the centers touch but there are gaps at the ends, one or both tables are low near the cutterhead. You only need to adjust the infeed table.

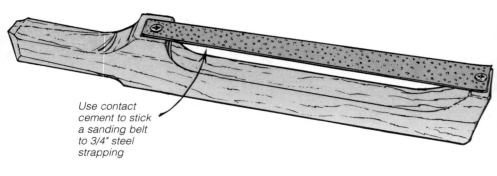

Use contact cement to stick a sanding belt to 3/4" steel strapping

Q&A

"I get very nervous routing

small parts, especially

those that bring my hands

within an inch or two of the

bit. Any ideas?"

Hot-melt glue a large

handle to a small part

before you approach the

router bit. Or you could glue

a piece of paper to the

workpiece with regular

yellow glue, and glue

a handle to the paper: this

makes it easy to take them

apart when you're done

routing. You'll only have to

do minor sanding.

Stiffen that Sanding Cloth

A sanding bow is great for curved surfaces, but sometimes it just isn't stiff enough. I glue the cloth to a strip of 3/4" steel strapping for greater control on intricate jobs.

Michael Burton
Glorieta, New Mexico

Masking Tape Eases Blade Changes

Here's an extremely basic suggestion for changing band saw blades, but one that is often overlooked. Just use a few short strips of masking tape to hold your band saw blade on the first wheel, while you thread it onto the second one.

Clifford Schwieger
Minneapolis, Minnesota

Reduce Scroll Saw Chipping

I use clear plastic laminate from an office supply store to reduce tearout when I scroll saw very thin stock. I just copy the pattern onto the laminate in a copy machine, then stick it to the wood.

Jack Williams
St. Joseph, Illinois

Winning the Air Hose Battle

For a long time I battled my 100-foot air hose every time I needed just a little more than my yellow coil hose could reach. But now I just pull as much hose as I need out of a 5-gallon pail. I drilled a 1" hole in the bottom for the male end to stick out and a 1" hole in the cover to push the hose in. Thread the male end through the cap and then through the bottom of the pail. Put the cap on the bucket, and push the rest of the hose in. Now you're all set to plug the male end of the hose into your air compressor and pull out as much hose as you need. The rest stays out of sight, and you don't have to buy an expensive hose coil.

Jim Galewski
Winona, Minnesota

Quick Tip

Every woodworker should get the chance to use a sharp, well-tuned hand plane. Begin tuning yours by removing the blade and flattening the bottom on a lapping plate. This is a piece of thick glass (3/8" or 1/2") with sandpaper glued to it. Use the lapping plate to flatten the back of the cutting iron, too, before you sharpen the front of it. Use a honing guide to re-establish the 30° bevel on the iron, then grind a second (27°) bevel with an aluminum oxide wheel on the grinder. After assembling the plane, lubricate the sole often with paraffin wax.

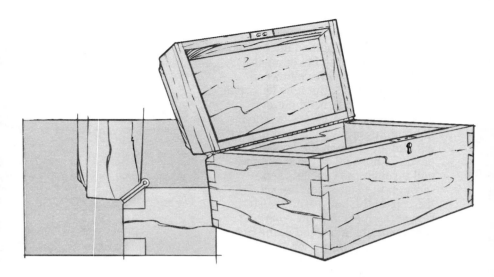

Q&A

"What temperature should my shop be for finishing?"

According to finishing specialist Jerry TerHark, there are three rules for finishing: the room should be 72°. The finish should be 72°. And the wood should be 72°. Kidding aside, the main thing is to have these three components the same temperature, close to 72°.

A More Efficient Lid Support

Every time I built a box, installing the lid support made me cringe. Not only did the support add cost to the project, but it usually interfered with whatever I wanted to put inside the box. I have discovered an alternative to the lid support, especially on small boxes with lightweight lids. Cutting the lid and the box at an angle before setting the hinge makes for a self-supporting lid. Cutting 45° angles will keep the lid perpendicular to the box, but this is usually a little more than necessary and puts undue strain on the hinge and screws. In most cases, I find that 40° angles are sufficient.

Michael Burton
Glorieta, New Mexico

Thin that Glue

Cut your carpenter's glue on veneer projects with a little water, to improve its viscosity and drying time.

A. M. Benson
Houston, Texas

Removeable Tray Adds Versatility

Last year I built a workbench from plans in your magazine. I included T-slot tracks that allow different stops, guides and jigs to be attached to the bench: I'm currently using your clamp support jig for glue-ups, and the T-square jig for layouts and dado routing.

This year, I added a tool tray to my workbench. It runs the full length of the back of the bench, and is very handy on some hand tool intensive projects. But it tends to get in the way with bigger casework projects. Because of that, my design uses the T-slot system to make removing the tray a snap.

Joe Cormier
Peabody, Massachusetts

Quick Tip

Setting the iron on a hand plane can be a delicate process. The plane's mouth must be open enough to admit a plane shaving, but the smaller the opening the less tearout there will be. So a plane set for curly woods should have a very small opening with the cap iron barely set back from the cutting edge.

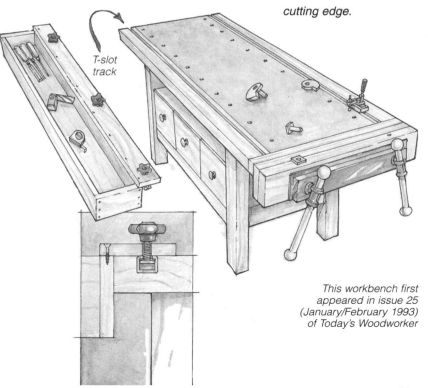

T-slot track

This workbench first appeared in issue 25 (January/February 1993) of Today's Woodworker

Q&A

"For some reason the section of veneer I think will look fantastic always comes up short in the final analysis. How do I select a better piece?"

Nature's paintbrush has created some truly astounding patterns in wood. When looking at a whole sheet of veneer, it's difficult to choose the exact piece of the pattern best suited to your project. Here's an old pro's trick to help you out: cut a hole the size of your substrate in a large piece of paper and move this around like a picture frame to select the most appealing pattern.

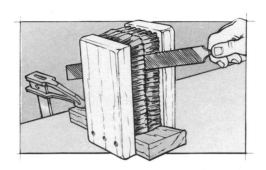

File and Rasp Cleaner

Sometimes I feel I spend more time cleaning out the wood particles that clog my rasps and files than I do shaping the wood. To remedy this, I took two inexpensive scrubbing brushes and trimmed off all the bristles 1" from one end of each. I screwed both brushes face to face on a 3/4" thick piece of pine that was just wide enough so the ends of the bristles met. Now all I have to do is saw the files and rasps down the middle, or move them in a figure eight for stubborn debris.

R. B. Himes
Vienna, Ohio

Loosen Up a Little

Never leave a tool with wooden threads screwed tight when it's not in use. Leave the threads loose to prevent damage from changes in humidity and resultant wood movement. For similar reasons, router bits should always be removed from the collet after you have finished working with them. If you don't, you risk having the bit rust to the collet or get locked in by resins.

Hugh Foster
Manitowoc, Wisconsin

Quick Tip

Knee-activated Safety Switch

This simple addition to my table saw required less than $6 in materials and took about 30 minutes to complete. It allows me to safely hit the OFF switch with my knee or shin without having to grope blindly while my hands are still holding the stock. A light tap anywhere on the 1/2" PVC frame does the trick, and the large open frame doesn't obstruct access to the ON switch or the blade height crank. My saw is a Grizzly Cabinetmaker; however, most any make can be accommodated with slight alterations to the basic scheme.

J. D. Carlson
Cary, North Carolina

If you're asked to build a cigar humidor, you should know that cigars are hygroscopic: they dry out when the surrounding humidity level falls and absorb too much moisture when it rises. A dry cigar burns too quickly, and the smoke is hot and acrid. A moist cigar is hard to draw on, with heavy smoke and a tart aroma.

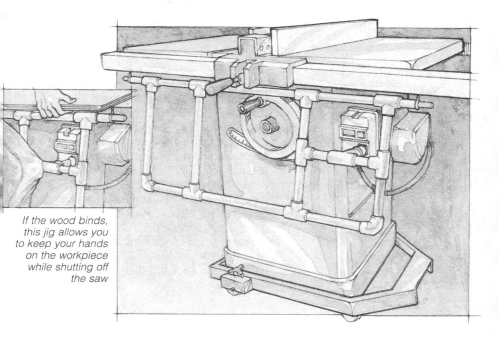

If the wood binds, this jig allows you to keep your hands on the workpiece while shutting off the saw

Q&A

"What kind of casters will let me move machines around the shop?"

Generally, the ideal setup is to have two fixed casters at one end of the machine, and two swivel casters at the other. That way, you can steer in much the same fashion as an automobile. All four should be locking, so the machine is stable in use. They should also be sized correctly: casters are rated as to the weight they can carry, so four 30 lb. casters can, in combination, tote a total of 120 lbs. Err on the side of caution and use heavier casters than you really need.

Improved Router Pad

I improved my pad for routing and sanding small pieces by stapling it tightly over a 1/4" plywood base. Now it is always ready to use, stays wrinkle free and, more importantly, doesn't have a tendency to oscillate or slide when I sand small pieces with my oscillating sander. The portion of the pad stapled under the perimeter of the plywood base keeps the pad stable on my workbench.

Dick Dorn
Oelwein, Iowa

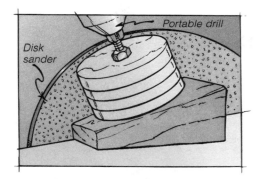

Making Perfectly Round Wheels

If you need a pair of wheels (or maybe even four), scribe circles on your stock and cut the wheels out on the band saw, staying just outside the lines. Drill a 1/4" hole at the center of each wheel, then slide the wheels onto a 1/4" threaded rod and tighten with nuts. Chuck the rod into your portable drill, clamp a wooden guide block onto the table of your disk sander and, with the drill in reverse, sand the wheels to their final size.

L. K. Bolay
Oak Harbor, Ohio

Image label: 2" x 4"

Storing Hand Screws

I've seen a variety of methods used to store hand screws (or parallel clamps). Most require returning the clamp to a holding position or some other setting. I drilled a 2" x 4" on edge with holes the size of the clamps' handles, and mounted it on the wall. When I'm done using them, I simply insert the clamp, rear handle first, into one of the holes. This way, the clamps can be stored in any open position and the holes can be just close enough for clearance, minimizing lost space.

John Kindseth
Lodi, California

Magnetic Vise Pads

Soft plastic business cards, intended as a refrigerator adornment, are given away by all kinds of businesses including realtors and insurance agents. They make excellent pads when used with steel clamps.

Joseph A. Fetchko
Ocean City, Maryland

Quick Tip

The safest way to resaw a board into two thinner boards is to run the board through the table saw on both edges to remove most of the waste, then finish up by separating the two halves on the band saw. A quick run through the thickness planer (or a short dance with a belt sander) and your boards are thin, flat and ready to go.

Q&A

"Why do hardwood plugs always show up so dark?"

The average hardwood plug is little more than a short length of dowel, so the part that is visible, after you've capped a screw and sanded it flush, is all end grain. This is a lot more porous than face grain, so it absorbs more stain and/or finish, hence its darker color. You can buy or make (with a plug cutter on the drill press) face grain plugs that blend in a little better. But sometimes if you can't totally hide something, it's better to show it off: plugs of a contrasting species may just be the way to go.

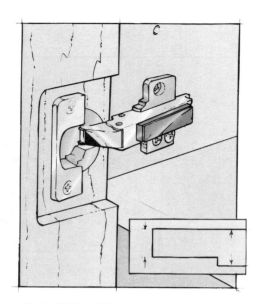

Retrofitting 1" Doors

I was retrofitting an old cabinet with cup hinges instead of the broken butt hinges that were on there, and ran into a problem when I discovered that the old doors were 1" thick. My standard hinges were for 3/4" thick doors. Instead of buying expensive replacement hinges designed for 1" doors, I just routed out an area a little larger than the cup and screw flange, reducing that small area to 3/4" thickness. I have found that this method works well on most inset doors: it presents a nice, clean look and will work for just about any door thickness.

Dennis DiVito
Buena Vista, Virginia

Save Your Glue

I use dish soap bottles for glue. If you won't be using them for a while, you can squeeze the air out.

Michael Vanderhorn
Bayonne, New Jersey

New Life for Cracked Blades

I have had several of my wider band saw blades — those over 1/4" in width — develop slight cracks, and have found that I can save them if the crack doesn't extend more than 1/6 of the way across the blade. I drill a very small hole with a #60 drill bit right at the bottom of the crack and the blade is ready to go back to work again.

Howard E. Moody
Upper Jay, New York

New Use for Post-it™ Notes

Marking the spot to drill for hardware on a freshly finished piece can by scary. Fresh finishes mar easily. Next time you're confronted with this dilemma, try placing a Post-it Note® in the approximate location of the intended hole and make your marks on that instead.

Michael J. Burton
Glorieta, New Mexico

Quick Tip

The three most popular band saw blades are the standard, skip and hook tooth. Standard blades have the most teeth and finest but slowest cuts. Skip tooth blades have half the number of teeth of a standard blade and cut faster but rougher. Hook tooth blades have evenly spaced, hooked teeth that are more aggressive yet.

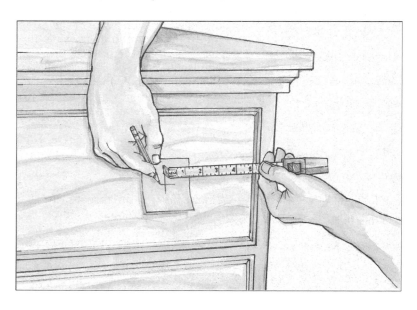

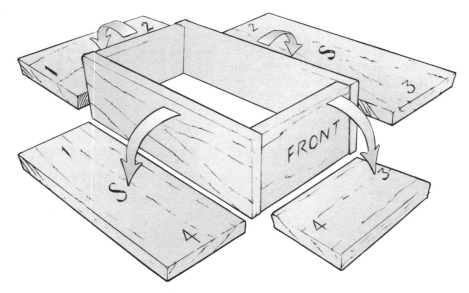

Q&A

"I see the guys on TV trim off their dowels and plugs with a strange-looking saw. Know where to get one?"

The saw you see is called a backsaw, and they are widely available in woodworking catalogs. The key to the one you're talking about is that the teeth have no set on one side, so they don't mar the work when used flush against it.

Placing Parts in the Dovetail Jig

I have over 30 years of woodworking experience and teach cabinetmaking and architectural woodworking at Utah Valley State College. As you can imagine, I have built and helped students build jillions of dovetailed drawers. One of the biggest problems students seem to have is keeping the parts in order and placing them correctly in the jig. The illustration above presents a simple system my students use to keep out of dovetail trouble.

Robert F. Steele
Orem, Utah

Screw Keeper

When changing the throat plate on my table saw, too frequently I dropped, lost or misplaced a screw. Now I bring a large magnet with me and stick all small metal parts to it.

Martha Dawson
Squaw Valley, California

Does your New Tape Measure Up?

When shopping for a tape measure, I open it up about six feet and double it over to see if all the incremental lines match up perfectly. Sometimes, it takes several shots before I find one that does.

Michael Carroll
Sacramento, California

Non-stick Drawer Guide

The drawer guide shown here is non-binding and has proved very practical after several years of use. The guide (A) is a piece of wood 1¹/₈" square, with a concave top. The groove is 3/4" wide and shallow enough that the drawer glides above the frame (B). The bottoms of the drawer sides are bullnosed to run in the groove, and the difference in the two arcs prevents binding when the wood dimensions change with the weather.

George H. Swisher
Bowie, Maryland

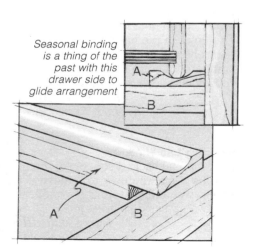

Seasonal binding is a thing of the past with this drawer side to glide arrangement

Quick Tip

Ok. The options are oil, ceramic and waterstones. Take your pick. That choice has become easier for woodworkers in recent years with huge improvements in the quality and array of waterstones. They are cleaner to work with than oilstones and don't permanently spot the wood. A diamond waterstone costs a little more, but it will remain flat and true with minimum maintenance (an occasional cleaning), give service life proportional to its cost, and be available in a wide range of sizes and grits. It can even be used to flatten your worn-out oilstones!

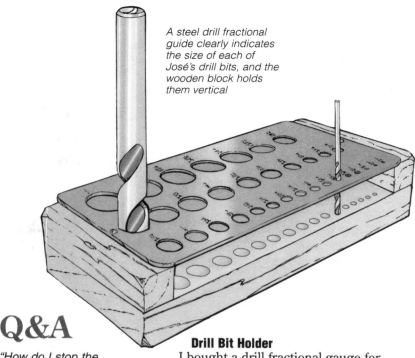

A steel drill fractional guide clearly indicates the size of each of José's drill bits, and the wooden block holds them vertical

Q&A

"How do I stop the bearing burn when I trim laminate?"

The pros like to spread a very thin coat of petroleum jelly on the bearing of their flush trim bit before tackling this task. It generally won't interfere with finishes and, if the bearing sticks a little, the petroleum jelly will release it. You can also soak the bearing (but not the screw!) in oil between uses.

Drill Bit Holder

I bought a drill fractional gauge for $2.97 from a mail order catalog. This is a 3" x 6" metal plate with holes ranging from 1/16" to 1/2", in 1/64" increments. I screwed the plate to two wood blocks glued to a wooden base, then drilled into the base using the gauge as a guide to make a 1/2" or 3/8" deep hole for each bit. The holes in the base hold the bits securely, and each bit is visibly numbered. I store them with the cutting end down for safety.

José A Mari Mutt
Mayaguez, Puerto Rico

But I Don't Do Windows

I use a metal-backed squeegee, the kind used for windows, to remove excess wood filler. Two coats of filler and two passes do a great job.

Harry Tuttle III
Wayzata, Minnesota

Mini Jig Knobs

Store bought knobs are too big for some jobs and often get in the way when used on my shop jigs. After failing to find smaller alternatives, I ended up making my own from electrical connection wire nuts and a handful of machine bolts. I removed the wire insert from each plastic nut cap by turning it counterclockwise with a screwdriver. Next, I filled the caps with epoxy and inserted the threaded end of machine bolts. Later, after the epoxy cured, I cut the bolts to length. Different sized wire nuts allowed me to use different thicknesses of machine bolts, all the way up to 1/4" diameter. Adding a rubber washer between the knob and jig increases the gripping strength.

Tony Wladyka
Mountainside, New Jersey

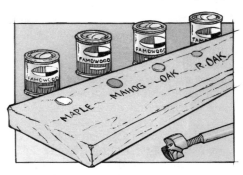

Wood Filler Color Template

Drill shallow holes with a small Forstner bit and fill them with every different wood putty you own, and you have an instant guide to what they'll look like dry, instead of depending on the color shown on the can.

Martin Kipp
Albany, New York

Quick Tip

If you don't own a drill press, keeping things vertical so the hole you drill is also vertical can be a problem. One way around this, at least for small parts, is to secure the part in a wooden handscrew clamp laid flat on the bench. The larger the clamp, the better. Clamp a pencil or drill bit in a second, smaller clamp and lay this on top of the first clamp. You now have a visual guide to help you keep the drilling operation vertical. You can even move it around to check from different angles. Just be sure the pencil truly is at 90° before you rely on it.

Q&A

"Do you have any tips for preparing a surface for prior to painting?"

We talked to Steve Jordan, the finishing expert at the Landmark Society in Rochester, New York, and he gave us these pointers. For shallow dents, polyester and epoxy fillers hold better than spackling or plastic woods. For a smooth finish on open grains, use a paste wood filler (not spackle) before priming. Whenever possible, keep the work surface horizontal, to avoid runs. And try tinting the primer the same color as your topcoat, for better coverage.

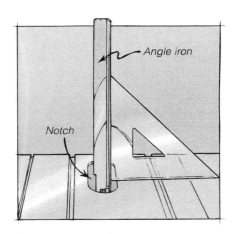

Setting Table Saw Stops

In setting up and checking the indicators on my table saw for 45° and 90°, I was always frustrated by the limitations imposed by using a saw blade as the guide. My solution is a 24" long section of extruded aluminum angle. It's inexpensive and widely available. To use it, begin by unplugging the saw! A 5/8" hole drilled a couple of inches up from one end allows you to replace the blade with the extrusion and secure it in place with the regular washer and nut. You may have to notch the extrusion to provide clearance for installation. Is that saw unplugged?

By using a 14" drafting triangle for setting the 45° and 90° angles, I now have a clear view and far more contact area. For intermediate angles, I use a machinist's protractor. A dial gauge between a flat metal bar in the miter slot and the aluminum extrusion provides a perfect parallel setting. Most angle extrusions are straight, but be sure to check yours anyway.

Robert England
Eugene, Oregon

Add Suction to your Radial Arm Saw

When I used to use my radial arm saw, the chips would fall on the table and floor. Fine dust would float in the air and get into the heating system, where it eventually found its way to the dining room table. My vacuum system never seemed to draw enough dust from the saw until I finally came up with this idea. The shield over the saw blade has an opening two inches wide and the air is divided across the whole expanse, leaving very little suction around the blade. The space is wide to accommodate a dado head and other cutters. All I did was fasten a piece of wood into the shield and around the hardware, and now I have plenty of suction.

James Johnson
Brunswick, Ohio

Quick Tip

If your tenons are just a hair too thick to fit in their mortises, try a traditional solution. You can shave them with a shoulder plane. That's a small metal plane (quite inexpensive and widely available) that essentially cuts across the grain, shaving the entire width of the plane.

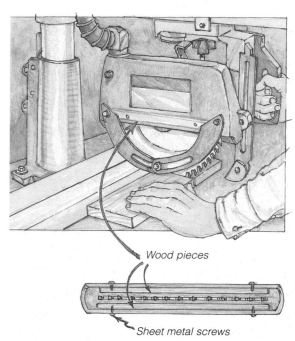

James Johnson mounted small wooden slats inside the blade aperture on his radial arm saw to reduce the airflow and increase the vacuum

Wood pieces

Sheet metal screws

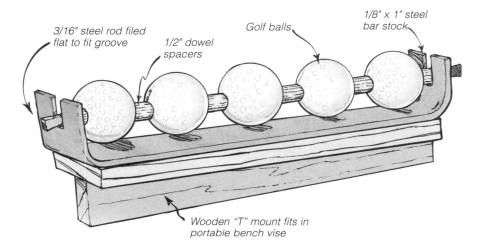

3/16" steel rod filed flat to fit groove

1/2" dowel spacers

Golf balls

1/8" x 1" steel bar stock

Wooden "T" mount fits in portable bench vise

Q&A

"What's good about shellac?"

Though modern finishes have relegated shellac to the back burner, it remains one of the most easily repaired finishes available. As a thin wash coat, it is unsurpassed for sealing pine and other porous woods, and it still dries in an hour or two. The layers meld together too, reducing any chance of failure.

Golf Ball Outfeed Rollers

As you can see from the sketch above, I've created a handy, affordable outfeed roller setup with nothing but materials I had on hand. I began by going through my golf bag and selecting five more or less junk balls with smiles or other defects. I drilled a 1/4" hole through each ball, as well as through the 1/2" dowel I used as spacers. Then I hacksawed a slot on each end of a thin steel bar, drilled mounting holes and bent the ends at 90°. A 3/16" steel rod was filed flat enough to slide snugly into the slots in the steel bar. Finally, all parts were assembled and mounted on a wooden "T" that I can clamp in my Workmate® at the right height for the outfeed of my saw.

P.S. Non-golfers shouldn't have any trouble getting used balls from golfing friends. Even if you have to buy used balls, they're very inexpensive.

R. B. Himes
Vienna, Ohio

Cork Sander Pads

The felt pad on my sander wore out, so I replaced it with two layers of 1/8" cork attached with contact cement. The cork wears longer, is flatter and doesn't rut as easily.

Dick Dorn
Oelwein, Iowa

A Shop-Built Router Stand

For safety reasons, I didn't like the idea of laying the router on its side, so I built this stand. I made it from 3/4" plywood and just glued everything together. I put carpet on the top for the router base to slide on. The 6" wide carpeted area is about 1/4" wider than the base of my router. This means I can slide my router on the stand while it's still coasting to a stop. The clearance below the router can be changed to match any length bit by just adding layers of plywood to the sides.

Richard G. Lobaugh
Chesterfield, Virginia

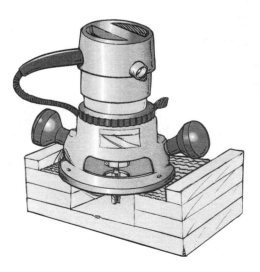

Quick Tip

Need to plane a small part? Then clamp your jack plane upside down in the end vise of your workbench. This way, the wood can be moved across the plane in full view, rather than trying to work on a part that is obscured by the body of the plane. If the part is so small that your fingers may contact the blade, then attach a handle to it. This handle can be a scrap of wood that is clamped on, or even one that is temporarily attached with hot-melt glue. Moving the wood rather than the plane has one other advantage: you can see when the mouth of the plane gets clogged, and where.

Closing Thoughts

If you liked what you found here ...

The tricks, tips, and jigs in this book were selected from back issues of Woodworker's Journal and Today's Woodworker magazine, (published from 1989 to 1998 and then merged with Woodworker's Journal).

*For more information about either magazine or our line of woodworking plans, please call us, toll-free, at **800-610-0883** or visit our web site:*

www.woodworkersjournal.com

Woodworker's Journal magazine:

Nearly the entire library of projects, covering almost 25 years, is available as individual reprints. Subscriptions to the magazine are available, as are subscriptions to our free online e-zine.

Rockler Woodworking and Hardware:

For Woodworking tools and supplies visit Rockler at rockler.com or call 1-800-279-4441.

Be Careful in Your Shop!

We at *Woodworker's Journal* have tried to make this book as accurate and correct as possible. The illustrations, diagrams and drawings, as well as the text, have been carefully researched by our in-house staff. However, due to the variability of local conditions, construction materials and personal skills, we assume no responsibility for any injuries, damages or other losses incurred that result from the material presented herein. All material presented should be carefully studied and clearly understood before attempting to duplicate techniques described.

For the sake of clarity, it is sometimes necessary for an illustration to show a power tool without its proper guards or safety equipment in place. In actual operation, always use the safety equipment provided with your tool by the manufacturer.

Notes

Treasured Recipes
of Country Inns

THE BERKSHIRE TRAVELLER COOKBOOK SHELF:

The Country Inn Cookbook
Wait A Minute . . . I'll Get You My Recipe
    By Carol Bergeron
You Can Save Money On That Meal
    By Carol Bergeron

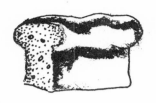

Treasured Recipes
of Country Inns

by

THE BERKSHIRE TRAVELLER

THE BERKSHIRE TRAVELLER PRESS
Stockbridge, Massachusetts 01262

Fifth Printing

Design: Janice Lindstrom
Library of Congress Catalog Card Number: 73-91008
ISBN 0-912944-08-0
Copyright © 1973 by The Berkshire Traveller Press

American Innkeeping dates back to the first few years after the landing of the Pilgrims. Early records show that the colony of Massachusetts found it desirable to have each town establish some kind of inn that would accommodate travelers and at the same time provide a meeting place for the villagers.

Today, personal innkeeping, personified by country inns, can be found in many parts of the world, providing unique accommodations and serving food that is frequently identified with its geographical location. It has been my experience that short of being a guest in a private home, country inns serve food that is closest to being "regional home cooking." With this thought in mind, I have persuaded a great many of the inns that have been included in our book, "Country Inns and Back Roads," to part with a favorite recipe, many representative of their region.

We've also included a word or two about the individual inns. The further story of our adventures is included in "Country Inns and Back Roads."

Even if you can't visit all of these inns personally, you can at least prepare their treasured recipes!

The Berkshire Traveller

CONTENTS

X DESSERTS

APPETIZERS
& SAUCES

BREAD AND BUTTER PICKLES

cucumbers, sliced very thin	1 gallon (after slicing)
onions, sliced thin	8 medium
green peppers, sliced thin	3
salt	1/2 cup
ice cubes	enough to bury vegetables

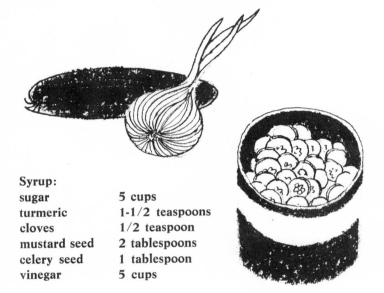

Syrup:

sugar	5 cups
turmeric	1-1/2 teaspoons
cloves	1/2 teaspoon
mustard seed	2 tablespoons
celery seed	1 tablespoon
vinegar	5 cups

Add salt to sliced vegetables and bury in ice cubes. Let stand 3 hours. Make syrup: heat all ingredients together, but do not boil. Drain vegetables, put into jars. Pour hot syrup over to cover them, and seal jars.

BETHEL INN
Bethel, Maine

The Inn is bright, orderly, highly polished and luxurious. Fresh flowers in every room are one of the ways guests feel the personal touch. Because of its sumptuous bedrooms, parlor and recreation rooms, its lawn and gardens, its well prepared food, I have taken many opportunities to recommend the Bethel Inn to other travellers.

TARTE AU FROMAGE DE VENCE

butter	2 tablespoons
flour	2 tablespoons
milk, scalded	1/2 cup
meat or vegetable stock	1/2 cup
processed gruyere cheese	1 6-ounce package
ham, diced and sauted	1/2 cup
egg yolks	2
rich pastry for tart shells	

Line small muffin tins with pastry; bake lightly, set aside. Melt butter, add flour, hot milk and stock; stir until thickened. Add cheese, stirring until melted; add sauted ham and remove from fire. Add egg yolks, beating quickly until blended. Fill tart shells and bake at 400 degrees, until filling is firm. Consistency will not be like a custard, but will be thick and chewy.

CHALET SUZANNE
Lake Wales, Florida

The Chalet is a conglomeration of small lodges, fantastic in their mingling of Oriental, Bavarian and Swiss architectural styles. It's like an imaginary village. I delighted in the details—cupolas, minarets, tiny bridges and many-shaped roofs. Chef Carl Hinshaw is also a pilot. His famous, European-inspired delicacies have long kept guests flying high!

13

ESCARGOTS MAISON

Marinade:

snails, with juice and shells	48
garlic, minced	1 clove
shallots, minced	1/4 cup
orange rind, sliced	1 orange
basil	1 teaspoon
tarragon	1 teaspoon
chervil	1 teaspoon
white wine	1/2-1 cup

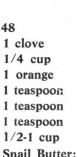

Snail Butter:

shallots, minced	3/4 cup
garlic, minced	5 cloves
parsley, chopped	1/2 cup
spinach, chopped	1 cup
Boston lettuce, chopped	1 cup
escarole, chopped	1 cup
chicory, chopped	1 cup
butter, at room temperature	2 sticks

Drain snails, reserving juice; add enough wine to make 1-1/2 cups liquid. Add other marinade ingredients and simmer 10 minutes. Pour hot liquid over snails, let cool, cover and refrigerate overnight. Snail butter: An hour before serving, pour marinade liquid into saucepan. Add all other ingredients except butter, cover and simmer very slowly 30 minutes, stirring occasionally. Cool; add butter and mix until creamy. Put about 1/2 teaspoon snail butter into each shell, add snail and fill to top with more snail butter. Bake 5-10 minutes at 400 degrees, until snail butter is bubbling. Serves eight for first course or six as main course.

CHESTER INN
Chester, Vermont

I visited Audrey Patterson's kitchen, enjoying dinner vicariously before the actual eating. This Vermont village inn is comfortable; however, it is the cuisine people remember.

KING CRABMEAT DIP

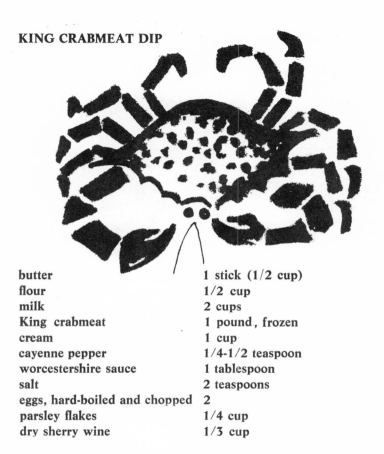

butter	1 stick (1/2 cup)
flour	1/2 cup
milk	2 cups
King crabmeat	1 pound, frozen
cream	1 cup
cayenne pepper	1/4-1/2 teaspoon
worcestershire sauce	1 tablespoon
salt	2 teaspoons
eggs, hard-boiled and chopped	2
parsley flakes	1/4 cup
dry sherry wine	1/3 cup

Thaw crabmeat and drain well. Melt butter over medium heat; add flour, mixing well. Stir in milk and continue stirring until sauce thickens. Add remaining ingredients and cook until heated thoroughly, stirring occasionally. Pour into chafing dish and serve as dip, with crackers or melba toast.

GENERAL LEWIS INN
Lewisburg, West Virginia

The General Lewis serves this elegant dip at parties. It is a bit of a change from the more traditional Southern menu. West Virginia's rich history is written on the Inn, which is almost entirely furnished in antiques. Broad lawns and Southern gardens complete the picture.

GRAMMY'S TOMATO JUICE

tomatoes, well ripened, quartered	1 peck
celery, including leaves, chopped	1/2 bunch
onions, chopped coarsely	4 medium
sugar	3 cups
salt	6 teaspoons

Crush tomatoes slightly. Simmer with celery and onions until vegetables are tender. Run through a colander. Add sugar and salt; bring to boil. Seal in sterilized jars. Makes about six quarts.

INN AT SAWMILL FARM
West Dover, Vermont

This rich tomato juice might be just the thing to prepare the palate for one of Chef Bill William's many glamorous, delicately prepared dishes. Like the cuisine, this resort-inn is a blending of textures—weathered wood, bricks and stone, complemented by the innkeeper's decorating skills. West Dover sits in easy view of Mt. Snow, so the Inn's hospitality often extends to Alpine and cross-country skiers.

COCKTAIL SAUCE

ketchup	2 cups
tomato paste	2 tablespoons
horseradish	1-1/2-2 tablespoons
curry powder	1/2 teaspoon
garlic powder	1/8 teaspoon
tabasco sauce	1/8 teaspoon
lemon juice	small lemon

Blend ingredients well; correct seasoning and horseradish for desired tang. Serve with Michigan whitefish, Mackinaw trout, Coho salmon, smoked chubs, or use your imagination. Also delicious with shrimp or scallops.

LEELANAU HOMESTEAD
Glen Arbor, Michigan

This tangy sauce would be a delightful accompaniment to the "Seafood-Stuffed Tomato." The Leelanau serves it with fish from nearby Lake Michigan. What a place to enjoy fish! The Inn is situated near the Sleeping Bear Dunes National Lakeshore. I could see Sleeping Bear Bay, the dunes, hardwood forests and the Manitou Islands, without leaving the premises.

HOLLANDAISE SAUCE FOR EGGS BENEDICT

butter	1/2 cup, scant
egg yolks	3
lemon juice	1 tablespoon
flour	1 heaping tablespoon
water,boiling	1 cup
salt	1/4 teaspoon
red pepper	1/4 teaspoon
mayonnaise	3 tablespoons

Melt butter in heavy saucepan over low heat. Beat egg yolks and add to melted butter very slowly, stirring constantly; add flour slowly, then boiling water, very slowly. Add lemon juice and red pepper; stir until mixture thickens. Set aside to cool. Add mayonnaise and serve. This sauce should be zippy: add extra lemon juice and pepper if necessary.

LINCKLAEN HOUSE
Cazenovia, New York

I lunched in one of the little side dining rooms that make the Lincklaen atmosphere especially intimate. There was a merry fire in the imposing fireplace, providing welcome warmth against the thick December snow outside. This spirited Hollandaise is a favorite of guests, who have compared it to New Orleans cooking—a fine compliment, indeed.

PEAR RELISH

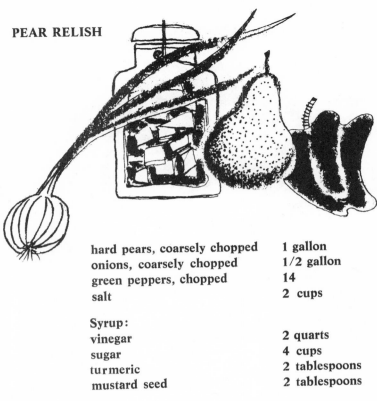

hard pears, coarsely chopped	1 gallon
onions, coarsely chopped	1/2 gallon
green peppers, chopped	14
salt	2 cups
Syrup:	
vinegar	2 quarts
sugar	4 cups
turmeric	2 tablespoons
mustard seed	2 tablespoons

Mix pears, onions and green peppers; add salt, let stand overnight. In the morning, drain and rinse four times in clear water, then drain until dry. Prepare syrup: cook all ingredients together 5 minutes; add chopped vegetable mixture and simmer another 5 minutes. Pour in hot jars and seal.

NU-WRAY INN
Burnsville, North Carolina

There's little time to dawdle at this inn. Guests are awakened early by the innkeeper's bell for a huge, congenial, family-style country breakfast. The bell rings again for the day's second meal, dinner. Missing it means starving until next morning. Antique furnishings at the Nu-Wray emphasize the unusual: old-fashioned door keys, to be hung on an old-fashioned rack in the lobby, rockers, a fireplace, and a "Regina" music box.

SEAFOOD STUFFED TOMATOES

smoked whitefish, flaked	1 pound
haddock, flaked	2 pounds
celery, chopped fine	1 bunch
onion, chopped fine	1 small
parsley, chopped fine	2 tablespoons
lemon juice	2 teaspoons
mayonnaise	1 cup
tomatoes	12 large
lettuce	12 leaves

Combine all ingredients except tomatoes. Then cut each tomato into wedges, leaving the wedges attached at the bottom; open each tomato on a plate and place about 1/12 of the salad mixture in the center. Serve on lettuce leaf with cocktail sauce garnish if desired.

OLD RED MILL
Clarence, New York

Hungry guests are served in a circa 1910 dining car, complete with red carpets and swinging lamps. The menu is a reproduction of an old-time railroad ticket. I made my selection by punching a hole next to my chosen dish. How delightful to find real country atmosphere just a short drive from the roar and bustle of the New York State Thruway!

CHILI RELLENOS

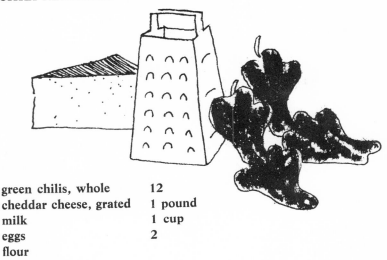

green chilis, whole	12
cheddar cheese, grated	1 pound
milk	1 cup
eggs	2
flour	

Stuff the chilis with grated cheddar cheese. Roll them in flour and dip into egg and milk batter. Fry in butter until golden brown on both sides. Serve immediately. Serves 4.

SAGEBRUSH INN
Taos, New Mexico

Myron and Muriel Vallier are from New Hampshire but the Sagebrush Inn is about as New England a country inn as will ever be found in New Mexico. However, the architecture is Spanish-colonial and the building and lodging rooms are all built of adobe brick. The rugs, wall hangings, door latches, doors, lamps are unquestionably New Mexico. If I can't be in Taos when I'm in the Berkshires, at least I can make this marvelous New Mexican dish and enjoy the memory of good food at the Sagebrush Inn.

TOMAT

SOUPS

BEAN SOUP

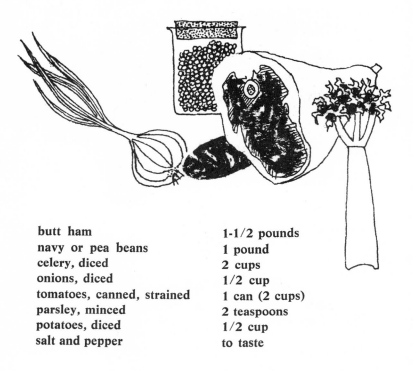

butt ham	1-1/2 pounds
navy or pea beans	1 pound
celery, diced	2 cups
onions, diced	1/2 cup
tomatoes, canned, strained	1 can (2 cups)
parsley, minced	2 teaspoons
potatoes, diced	1/2 cup
salt and pepper	to taste

Cover beans with water and soak overnight. Cook in same water until almost soft. Wash ham, cover with cold water, and cook until tender. Remove ham from pot; add the beans and remaining ingredients to ham broth and cook together slowly until tender. Serve ham sliced, separately from soup. Serves ten-twelve.

BROMLEY HOUSE
Peru, Vermont

Skiers might welcome this robust soup, but it would please anyone, in any season. I try to visit Bromley House often; it is a welcome friend and an old one, set comfortably in the Vermont mountains.

24

VICHYSSOISE

potatoes, cooked and thinly sliced	1-1/2 cups
shallots, finely sliced	2 tablespoons
chicken broth	2 cups
salt	1/2 teaspoon
white pepper	dash
worcestershire sauce	1-1/2 teaspoons
bay leaf, whole (a must)	1
heavy cream	2-3 cups
chives, freshly minced	1-2 tablespoons

Combine all ingredients except cream and chives and simmer slowly about 2 hours, until mixture is thickened to the consistency of mashed potatoes. Remove bay leaf and cool. Add to blender equal parts of cream and mixture, blending thoroughly. More or less cream may be added, according to whether you prefer a thicker or a thinner vichyssoise. Sprinkle with chives and serve ice cold.

CLARKSON HOUSE
Lewiston, New York

This carefully seasoned version of an old favorite would be a lovely preface to one of the substantial meat dishes featured at this country restaurant. Steaks and chops are prepared on a grill, placed in the center of the warm, antique-laden dining room. To top it all off, Clarkson House is only 7 miles from Niagara Falls, an ideal dinner stop for visitors to that age-old vacation spot.

HILDA COPPAGE'S LOBSTER STEW

live lobsters	4, 1-1/2 pounds each
salt	1 tablespoon
sugar	1 teaspoon

Stock:	
clam juice	1 pint
water	1 pint
parsley	1 sprig
celery	1 stalk
carrot	1
bay leaf	1
onion, stuck with 2 cloves	1

Sauce:	
butter	2 tablespoons
flour	1-2 tablespoons
salt	to taste
pepper, freshly ground	1/8 teaspoon or more
nutmeg	1/8 teaspoon
cayenne pepper	1/8 teaspoon
dry sherry	about 1/2 cup
cream	2 pints

Boil lobsters 15 minutes in water with salt and sugar added; leave claw meat whole; cut tail in large chunks and set aside. Simmer bodies in ingredients for stock. Saute meat in butter at low heat; sprinkle lightly with flour, salt, pepper, nutmeg, cayenne and sherry. Add 1 cup broth (do not strain any liver or roe), and then add cream. Taste for seasoning: add more sherry, if desired. Heat gently. Serve with small, hot, buttered and toasted Westminster common crackers.

COONAMESSET INN
Falmouth, Massachusetts

Beautiful flowers and equally beautiful food abound at this handsome Cape Cod inn. The lobster stew belongs to the Bouillabaisse and Cippino family of meal-in-one seafood soup-stews.

CHEESE SOUP

onion, chopped fine	1 small
butter or margarine	2 tablespoons
flour	1/4 cup
sherry	1/2 cup
chicken stock or bouillon	2 cups
strong Vermont cheese	2 tablespoons
parmesan cheese, grated	1/4 cup
milk	1 cup
cream	1 cup
parsley, chopped	to taste
chives, chopped	to taste

Saute onion in butter until golden brown. Add flour and stir until smooth. Add chicken stock and sherry; strain at once. Cook slowly, adding both kinds of cheese, stirring until melted. Bring to a gentle boil, adding more cheese if desired. Add milk and cream, heat and serve. (Do not boil again.) More milk may be added, if thinner soup is desired. Serves four-six.

GREEN MOUNTAIN INN
Stowe, Vermont

This is a fine, smooth soup that complements the Inn's solid New England cooking. I prefer the tranquility of a summertime visit because of the heavy winter traffic on nearby ski slopes. The Inn is six miles from Mt. Mansfield, highest peak in Vermont's Green Mountains.

KALE SOUP

beef shin bone, well meated	2 pounds
peppercorns	6
salt	2 teaspoons
bay leaf	1
garlic	2 cloves
onions	2 medium
chorizo (very hot)*, skinned and chopped	1 pound
Linguica (hot)*, skinned and chopped	1 pound
fresh kale, chopped	1 bunch (or 2 pkgs. frozen)
shell or horticultural beans, slightly crushed	1 can
potatoes, peeled and diced	1-1/2 pounds

*These are Portuguese sausages; Kielbasa or any highly spiced sausage will do as a substitute.

In heavy stock pot, place shin bones, peppercorns, salt, bay leaf, garlic and onions, cover with 4 quarts water and simmer 2 hours. Add sausages, kale and beans; simmer 1/2 hour. Add potatoes and continue simmering until done. Remove from heat. Remove bones and when cool, remove meat from the bones, breaking it up if necessary; put meat back in pot, with marrow from bones. Refrigerate overnight to blend the flavors. Heat and serve with garlic-buttered Portuguese or French bread, a large spoon, and a napkin for under the chin. Freezes perfectly, if you have leftovers.

HARBORSIDE INN
Edgartown, Massachusetts

I was up just after dawn, watching the Edgartown Harbor wake up to an early autumn day. The Harborside is right on the water, to the seaward side of Martha's Vineyard. The Kale Soup has strong overtones of nearby Cape Cod's Portuguese heritage. It is excellent served with fresh fish or seafood, but it can well be a meal in itself.

SEAFOOD CHOWDER

milk	3 cups
salmon*	1 cup
mushroom soup	1 can
butter	1 tablespoon
cream	1 1/2 cups
lobster	1 small can
onion	1
green pepper	1/4
celery	1 stalk
salt, pepper	to taste
shrimp	1 small can

Chop onion, celery, green pepper and saute lightly in butter.
Combine the onion, celery, and green pepper with the other
ingredients; salt and pepper to taste. Bring to a scald. A
touch of sherry may be added just before serving.

* Any fish may be added or substituted in this recipe.

INVERARY INN
Baddeck, Cape Breton, Nova Scotia

The Inverary Inn is a bonnie bit of Scotland on the shores of
Lake Bras D'or. Besides superb oat cakes, this seafood chowder
and other Cape Breton specialties are making Innkeeper Isobel
MacAulay well known in all parts of the United States and
Canada.

ALPINE CHEESE SOUP WITH DILL

raw lean bacon, diced	4 slices
onion, diced	1/2 medium
celery, diced	1 stalk
leek, diced	1
rolled oats	1/2 cup
salt	1 teaspoon
pepper	1/2 teaspoon
chicken stock, fresh (or use canned broth and eliminate salt from recipe)	6 cups
Swiss gruyere cheese, grated	1/2 cup
sharp cheddar, grated	1/2 cup
heavy cream	1/4 cup
Kirsch (or white wine)	1/4 cup
dill, fresh or dried, chopped	1 tablespoon

Saute bacon 3 minutes, in heavy 4-quart saucepan. Add onion, leek and celery; saute until tender. Add oats, salt, pepper and stock. Simmer uncovered 40 minutes, over low heat; remove from heat. Puree soup in blender until smooth. Return to saucepan, over low heat; add cheese slowly, stirring until melted. Add cream and stir; add Kirsch. Do not boil again. Taste for seasoning. Serve sprinkled with chopped dill. Serves four-six.

PUMP HOUSE INN
Canadensis, Pennsylvania

The Pump House boasts one of the most unusual interiors I have seen—a lovely , indoor waterfall in its well endowed dining room. The food is unusual as well. Chef Bill Cardwell's French provincial specialties have earned him well-deserved fame.'

COLD CUCUMBER SOUP

leeks, chopped fine	1/4 cup
onions, chopped fine	1/4 cup
celery, chopped fine	1/4 cup
cucumbers, peeled, seeded, and chopped	3
butter	
sherry	1/4 cup
chicken stock	2 cups
roux *	to thicken
salt, pepper	to taste
sesame seeds, dry mustard, thyme, chervil	a pinch
light cream	1 pint
orange juice	1/4 cup

Saute the leeks, onions, celery, and cucumbers in butter. Add sherry, chicken stock and seasonings and let cook 20 minutes. Add roux to thicken; then add light cream. Cook 15 minutes and cool. Add the orange juice and serve cold.

*roux — a mixture of melted butter and flour used to thicken soups and sauces.

RED LION INN
Stockbridge, Massachusetts

The Red Lion always has three soups on the menu. This cold cucumber soup is one of the most popular. A perfect soup for a Berkshire summer day.

CHILLED AVOCADO SOUP

avocados, ripe	enough to make 2-3 cups pulp
milk	1 cup
cream	1 cup
chicken broth, canned	2 cups
onion, minced	1 tablespoon
worcestershire sauce	1/4 teaspoon
sour cream	2 tablespoons
salt and pepper	to taste

Remove pulp from avocado shells. Put part of pulp, broth and milk-cream mixture in blender with onion and worcestershire sauce. Blend well, repeating until balance of ingredients has been used up. With wire whisk, fold in sour cream, salt and pepper. Mix well; seal container tightly and chill thoroughly. Skim off any discoloration that may occur on top of mixture. Garnish with chopped parsley or paprika. Serves six.

1740 HOUSE
Lumberville, Pennslyvania

In the heart of Bucks County I found what one guest called "The most romantic country inn. . ." Each room has its own balcony, overlooking both river and canal. This cool avocado soup is only one of many mouth-watering dishes that make up the varied menu.

32

SQUASH BISQUE

onion, minced	1 small (1/4 cup)
butter	2 tablespoons
frozen potato soup, thawed	1 can
water	1-1/2 cups
squash	1 cup
light cream	1 cup
pepper	1/4 teaspoon
nutmeg	1/4 teaspoon

Saute onion in butter until soft; stir in potato soup. Heat, stirring occasionally. Stir in squash, cream, pepper, nutmeg and simmer 20 minutes. Float sour cream or thin slices of raw zucchini on top.

STAFFORD'S BAY VIEW INN
Petoskey, Michigan

Little Traverse Bay is a good place to focus a trip through northern Michigan. Bay View has been a summer cultural center for many years. At the Inn, visitors can read and relax, or they can partake of water sports, musical, religious and other summer events, or the fine winter skiing. This gently seasoned bisque is adaptable to any meal, any time of year.

PEANUT SOUP

chicken or turkey stock	**3 cups**
peanut butter	**2 cups**
milk or cream	**1 cup**
onion, diced	**1 medium**
celery, diced	**1 stalk**
carrot, diced	**1**
salt and pepper	**to taste**

Add stock, onion, celery and carrots to peanut butter. Add milk or cream, salt and pepper, and blend thoroughly. Heat but do not boil.

WAYSIDE INN
Middletown, Virginia

Set in the lush green of the Shenandoah Valley, the Wayside dates from at least 1797. In keeping with the Inn's longevity, five generations of cooks make up chef Irene Washington's family history. The Peanut Soup is one of the most unusual of the Southern dishes. I also sampled two kinds of ham and noted such delectables as southern fried chicken, beef burgundy, duck a l'orange and shrimp creole on the menu. Spoon bread is another specialty of the house.

CHEESE
& EGGS

GRITS CASSEROLE

water, boiling	2 cups
salt	1/2 teaspoon
hominy grits	1/2 cup
margarine	1/2 stick
garlic cheese	1/2 roll
egg, beaten	1
tabasco sauce	dash (1/8 teaspoon)
cornflake crumbs	1/2 cup

Cook grits in salted water as directed; add margarine and cheese and stir until melted. Add beaten egg, mix well, and pour into buttered casserole. Cover with cornflake crumbs, dot with butter; bake 15-20 minutes at 400 degrees.

DOE RUN INN
Brandenburg, Kentucky

Grits are a southern dish many Yankees are afraid of. This luscious casserole is a good introduction for the timid. I can really rest at Doe Run, without television or even a phone in my room. The inn has quite a history. Abe Lincoln's father helped to build the original structure. Today, visitors can wander the huge forest that still surrounds the building.

THE FARMER'S OMELET

ham, diced fine	2 slices
hot dog, diced fine	1
bacon, diced fine	1 slice
onion, diced fine	5 ounces
potato, cooked, cold, diced	1/2 medium
eggs, beaten	3

Saute diced vegetables and meats until tender and lightly browned. Pour off excess fat; add to eggs. Over medium heat, mix rapidly and form into omelet. Serves one.

LORD JEFFERY INN
Amherst, Massachusetts

This omelet would get any farmer off to a good, early start. The Lord Jeff serves a wide variety of guests, because of its location in a five-college area. It is a good town in which to browse in any of several shops.

HAM, MACARONI, TOMATO AND CHEESE CASEROLE

elbow macaroni	1/2 pound
ham, cooked, diced	1 cup
tomatoes, diced	1 cup
milk	1 cup
sharp cheese, grated	3 ounces
egg	1

Cook macaroni in salted, boiling water until soft. Drain in colander. In a well-greased casserole, alternate layers of macaroni, cheese, ham and tomatoes. Beat egg and milk together; pour over top. Set casserole in pan of hot water and bake 30-40 minutes at 350 degrees.

OLD CLUB RESTAURANT
Alexandria, Virginia

George Washington didn't sleep here, but he did eat here. He and a group of friends built the original part of this colonial house as a private club. The recipe makes a good, basic, hearty dinner.

SCRAMBLED EGGS SUTTER CREEK STYLE

scallions, diced	3
chicken fat	1 teaspoon
rich cream	1/4 cup
eggs	14
mushrooms, thickly cut	1-2 cups
garlic powder	1 teaspoon
mixed herb seasoning*	1-3 teaspoons

Cook mushrooms lightly; sprinkle with garlic powder and set aside. Lightly fry scallions in chicken fat. Beat eggs with cream; toss in hot pan and cook quickly. Serve with mushrooms in center of eggs, on large platter; sprinkle with herb seasoning. Serves six.

*preferably Villa de Vero, put out by Gourmet Spices Ltd., Fulton, Calif.

SUTTER CREEK INN
Sutter Creek, California

These are truly elegant scrambled eggs. The inn is small and intimate; guests often return many times. Primarily for adults, Sutter Creek is a good place to center an exploration of Gold Rush Country.

MEATS

SHORT RIBS

short ribs, "choice" grade	8 8-ounce portions
salt	to taste
red pepper seeds	to taste
onions, chopped	2 large
green peppers, chopped	2
tomatoes, stewed (canned), and chopped	2 large
apricot jam or preserves	2 tablespoons
brown sauce	

Place ribs in pot, cover with water, season with salt and red pepper. Simmer until almost done. Rinse meat under cold water faucet, washing off excess fat. Dry meat, arrange in casserole, layering vegetables over meat, with onions first, then peppers, and finally tomatoes. Add apricot preserves, then brown in moderate oven (350 degrees). Add brown sauce to cover meat, return casserole to oven and bake at 350 degrees until meat is tender. Serve with oven-browned potatoes. Serves eight.

THE BOTSFORD INN
Farmington, Michigan

A quiet village inn in Detroit? I had to see it to believe it. Originally a stagecoach stop, the Botsford boasts of Henry Ford's own antiques. Chef George Kamen's hearty cooking includes several beef entrees, with these short ribs a favorite of guests.

SHISH KEBAB

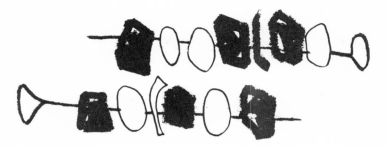

onion, chopped	2 tablespoons
olive oil	2 tablespoons
red wine vinegar	6 ounces
oregano	1 teaspoon
bay leaves, crushed	2
garlic, crushed	1 clove
salt and pepper	to taste
lean lamb, cut in chunks	1 1/2 pounds
tomatoes, small "cherry" type or large ones, quartered	about 8-12
onions, small or large, cut	about 8
mushrooms, whole fresh	about 8-12
green peppers, cut in 8 pieces	about 2

Brown chopped onion in olive oil. Remove from heat, add vinegar, oregano, bay leaves, garlic, salt and pepper. Marinate meat in this mixture at least 6 hours, turning occasionally. Thread meat onto long skewers, alternating with tomatoes, onions, mushrooms and peppers. Broil, turning once, about 15 minutes (depending on size of chunks, and how well done you like them). Serve very hot with rice pilaf.

COUNTRY SQUIRE
Killingworth, Connecticut

A good shish kebab is likely to please almost anyone. This recipe from one of New England's most charming inns is no exception. A light-hearted inn, the Squire has remained small and intimate over the years.

STUFFED PORK CHOPS, SHAKER APPLE DRESSING

pork chops, center cut	4 10-ounce

Dressing:

butter	3 tablespoons
white bread, dried and diced	1-1/2 cups
celery, diced	1/2 cup
sage	1/2 teaspoon
thyme	1/8 teaspoon
pepper	1/8 teaspoon
eggs	2
onions, diced	1/2 cup
basil	1/2 teaspoon
salt	1/4 teaspoon
chicken bouillon	1/4 cup or more
apples, peeled, cored, sliced	2 medium

Broth:

pork stock or bouillon	1-2 cups
onions, diced	2
celery, diced	2 stalks
carrots, diced	2
peppercorns	1 teaspoon
bay leaf	1

Melt butter, saute onions and celery; add to bread. Add eggs, then all herbs, salt, pepper and apples. Add 1/4-1/2 cup bouillon and mix. Make pocket in pork chop; sprinkle with salt and pepper, brown in skillet. Stuff pocket with dressing, place chops on rack in covered roasting pan. Cover bottom of pan with pork stock or bouillon, vegetables and seasonings. Bake 45-60 minutes at 350 degrees, basting occasionally. Remove cover from pan last 10 minutes to brown chops. Strain broth and discard vegetables; make gravy from broth, by stirring in roux (flour and butter) and heating, to desired thickness. Serves four.

THE GOLDEN LAMB
Lebanon, Ohio

I love Christmas at this warm Ohio inn. I also love stuffed pork chops, and other Golden Lamb delicacies, any time of year.

CHINESE GREEN PEPPER STEAK

filet mignon, cubed	about 1 pound
green pepper, sliced	1
celery tips, sliced diagonally	4
onion rings, halved	3-4
tomato, cubed	1
soy sauce	4 tablespoons

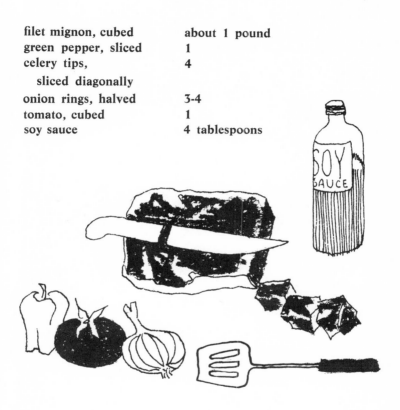

Saute celery, onions and green pepper until tender but not overcooked. Add semi-cooked filet, then soy sauce. Just before serving, add tomato, serve over rice. Serves four.

HOVEY MANOR
North Hatley, Quebec

The inn is quite a surprise. Built by an American from Atlanta, it offers the elegance and charm of a Southern mansion, in the lush, natural setting of rural Quebec. With all the cultural minglings I was hardly surprised to see a Chinese dish on the menu.

ENDIVES AND HAM IN MORNAY SAUCE

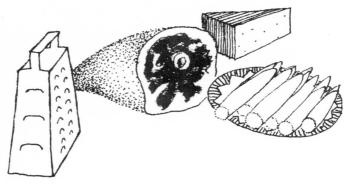

endives, braised (or cooked asparagus)	8
lean boiled ham, sliced thin	8 slices
Sauce Mornay:	
butter	4 tablespoons
flour	4 tablespoons
milk	1-1/2 cups
cream	1 cup
white pepper, freshly ground	to taste
salt	to taste
Swiss cheese, grated	1/2 cup

Wrap each endive in a slice of ham. Place in well buttered baking dish. Cover with sauce Mornay, sprinkle with cheese, dot with butter. Bake about 25 minutes at 400 degrees, until nicely browned. Serve with French bread.

KILRAVOCK INN
Litchfield, Connecticut

I thought I saw a Scottish manor house in the rolling Litchfield hills. Kilravock (pronounced "Kil-rook") is a picture book inn, with a menu fit for a king. The endives and ham are easy to prepare, but elegant enough to please the most seasoned gourmet.

LYME INN WIENER SCHNITZEL

fresh veal tenderloin	12 ounces
bread flour	4 ounces
salt	pinch
fresh bread crumbs	4 ounces
eggs	2
butter-flavored oil	2 ounces
fresh butter	2 ounces
fine capers	1 tablespoon

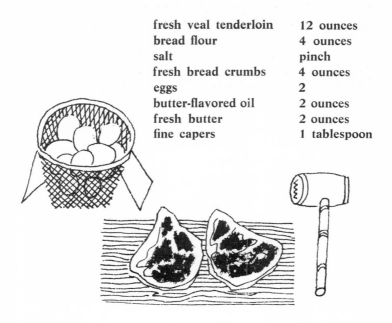

Divide veal into two pieces and flatten it on meat board until 1/4-inch thick. Sprinkle pinch of salt over veal, place in flour and pat gently on both sides. Scramble egg in small bowl. Submerge veal in egg, then dip in bread crumbs and pat lightly on both sides. Heat oil in heavy pan; add veal and saute until golden brown. Remove veal from pan; pour out oil. Add butter, and return to pan. Let stand 5 minutes in hot pan with no heat. Sprinkle with capers; serve at once. Garnish with piece of lemon. Serves two.

LYME INN
Lyme, New Hampshire

Fresh fish from the nearby Connecticut River join dishes like this handsome wiener schnitzel, to make up the large menu. The inn is precisely furnished and meticulously cared for.

MORGAN VEAL STEW

stewing veal	2 pounds
flour	
salt and pepper	to taste
pork drippings	1/4 cup
onions, chopped	1/4 cup
fresh parsley, chopped	1/4 cup
fresh mushrooms, sliced	1 cup
chicken stock, hot	2 cups
sour cream	1 cup
white wine	1/2 cup
salt	1 teaspoon
worcestershire sauce	1 teaspoon
flour	1 tablespoon

Wipe veal and roll in flour, salt and pepper. Heat pork drippings in 2-1/2 quart Dutch oven. Place over very low heat, add onions, parsley, and mushrooms, cook until soft. Add veal and brown on all sides. Blend stock into sour cream and pour over veal. Add wine, salt and worcestershire sauce; mix well. Cover and bake 1-1/2 - 2 hours at 350 degrees, until tender. Stir occasionally. Thicken gravy with flour; serve with curried rice.

MORGAN HOUSE
Lee, Massachusetts

I think this recipe explains my attachment to the Morgan House dining room, although the atmosphere is nice, too. The lobby wall is papered with old register sheets. U.S. Grant is among the more famous visitors whose signatures appear. Lee is near Tanglewood and Jacob's Pillow.

HUNGARIAN BEEF GOULASH

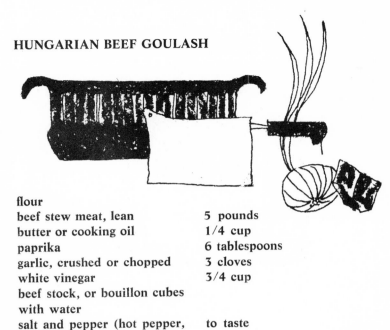

flour	
beef stew meat, lean	5 pounds
butter or cooking oil	1/4 cup
paprika	6 tablespoons
garlic, crushed or chopped	3 cloves
white vinegar	3/4 cup
beef stock, or bouillon cubes with water	
salt and pepper (hot pepper, if desired)	to taste
onions, sliced	5-6 medium (to equal volume of meat)

Saute garlic lightly in large casserole; add meat and brown thoroughly. Add onions and paprika, stirring to blend. Add vinegar, dust with flour, then bake 5-10 minutes at 375 degrees, until flour is lightly browned. Stir well; add enough stock to cover meat mixture; stir lightly, then bake until tender. Stock will reduce while cooking; more should be added, a little at a time. Season with salt and pepper and serve with buttered noodles or boiled potatoes. Sour cream may be added to top of casserole if desired.

MOUNTAIN VIEW INN
Norfolk, Connecticut

Goulash is basically stew—but no ordinary stew this. The Mountain View menu is extremely sophisticated, with many European delicacies as well as New England standbys like Boston scrod. Set in the Litchfield Hills, the inn is an easy drive from Hartford and the Massachusetts Berkshire region.

YANKEE POT ROAST

beef roast, bottom round	**5-6 pounds**
onion, coarsely chopped	**1 large**
salt	**1/2 teaspoon**
pepper	**1/8 teaspoon**
soy sauce	**6 tablespoons**

Brown meat on all sides in heavy skillet. Place in roasting pan. Add onion, salt, pepper, soy sauce; cover with hot water. Cover top with aluminum foil, then cover roasting pan with roaster cover. Bake 4 hours at 425 degrees. Reduce heat to 350 degrees and bake 1-2 hours more. Skim fat from broth and use broth for gravy, thickening with flour if desired.

NEW LONDON INN
New London, New Hampshire

Lake Sunapee is the setting for quiet New London, a college town surrounded by mountains. The innkeeper says a Yankee Pot Roast "seems to fit our old country inn." I agree.

CHILI CON CARNE

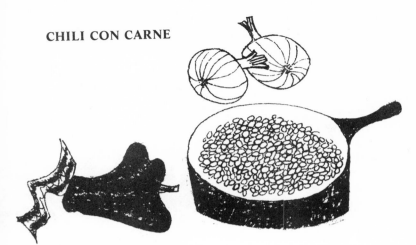

red kidney beans	1 pound
water	2 quarts
green chili pepper, chopped	3 tablespoons
tomato sauce	about 2 cups
salt	to taste
white pepper	1-1/2 teaspoons
bacon fat	1/2 cup
onions, sliced	2 medium-large
ground beef	2 pounds
garlic powder	1-1/2 teaspoons
chili powder	2 tablespoons
tomatoes, chopped	1 quart

Soak beans overnight, then cook in same water until tender. Drain and add chili pepper, salt, white pepper and tomato sauce. Let stand 2 hours. Heat onions, ground beef, garlic powder and chili powder in bacon fat; cook 30 minutes. Add tomatoes; cook 1 hour and serve.

RANCHO DE LOS CABALLEROS
Wickenburg, Arizona

Chili con carne represents the essence of Southwestern cooking. This luxury ranch-inn is set in the high desert, about an hour's drive north of Phoenix.

SWEETBREADS DES GOURMETS

sweetbreads	2 pair (2 pounds)
carrots, diced	2
onions, diced	2 medium
butter, clarified	2 tablespoons
dry white wine	1/2 cup
beef broth	1 cup
heavy cream	1/2 cup
mushrooms, sliced	4 large
artichoke bottoms, sliced	4
truffles	1 teaspoon
Madeira wine	2 tablespoons
arrowroot	1 teaspoon, scant

Blanch sweetbreads in 1 quart water, 1 tablespoon vinegar and .1 tablespoon salt. When boil is reached, plunge sweetbreads in cold water, remove. Clean by removing the tough outside membrane. In casserole, saute carrots and onions in butter until brown; add sweetbreads and brown lightly. Add white wine and cook uncovered until quantity of liquid is reduced by half. Add beef broth, cover casserole, braise 45 minutes. Place mushrooms and artichokes in a separate casserole with truffles, small amount of butter, and the Madeira wine. Set over low heat and let reduce by half. Remove sweetbreads and place in casserole with mushrooms, etc. Cook braising stock until reduced by half. Thicken with arrowroot mixed with heavy cream. Bring to boil; strain over casserole of sweetbreads. Cover and heat 15 minutes at 350 degrees. Serves four.

SWISS HUTTE
Hillsdale, New York

A rare recipe from an equally unusual, continental-style inn, tucked into a Berkshire valley near the New York-Massachusetts line.

SEAFOOD

BARNEGAT BAY STEW WITH DUMPLINGS

salt pork	3/4 pound
potatoes, cubed	5 medium
onions, sliced	3 medium
pepper	1 teaspoon
celery salt	2 teaspoons
bay leaves	4
thyme	1/2 teaspoon
clam broth	1-2 quarts
carrots, cubed	2 cups
flour	
clams	6 dozen
oysters	6 dozen
dumplings (may be made with mix)	

Brown salt pork. Pour off about 3/4 of the fat; add potatoes, onions and seasoning. Mix and saute 5 minutes. Cover mixture with clam broth or water and cook until potatoes are tender but still firm. Make a roux with flour and some of the broth, add to stew, stirring well. Add carrots, clams and oysters. Top with dumplings and cook 10 minutes, uncovered. Cover and cook 10 minutes more. Serve immediately.

AMERICAN HOTEL
Freehold, New Jersey

This sturdy seafood stew belongs to one of the largest and most varied menus I have ever seen. A large part of early American history happened near the hotel.

BAKED STUFFED FLOUNDER

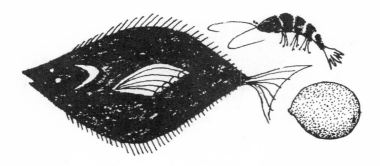

butter	1 cup plus 3 tablespoons
flour	3 tablespoons
milk, scalded	1 cup
shallots, chopped fine	4
shrimp, cooked	20 medium
crabmeat, cooked	8 ounces
lemon juice	to taste
dry white wine	to taste
salt and pepper	to taste
flounder, split, bone removed	4 12-ounce

Melt 3 tablespoons butter, add flour and mix thoroughly. Add milk and stir to a smooth sauce. Saute shallots in 1 cup butter. When lightly cooked to a blonde color, add shrimp and crabmeat mixture and season with lemon juice, white wine, salt and pepper. Fill each of the flounder with stuffing mixture; place in shallow baking dish. Bake 12-15 minutes at 400 degrees, until flounder is done.

BLACK POINT INN
Prouts Neck, Maine

Black Point Inn is a luxury resort-inn and this recipe attests to the luxury of its cuisine. My devotion to the inn is shared by many other guests, who enjoy the seaside activities and the genteel, old-time atmosphere.

KING CRABMEAT DELIGHT

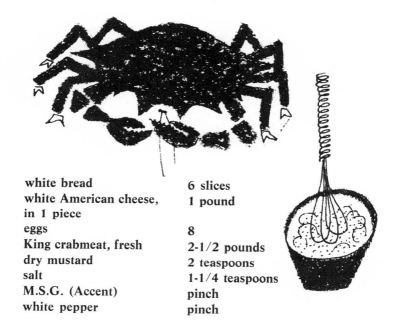

white bread	6 slices
white American cheese, in 1 piece	1 pound
eggs	8
King crabmeat, fresh	2-1/2 pounds
dry mustard	2 teaspoons
salt	1-1/4 teaspoons
M.S.G. (Accent)	pinch
white pepper	pinch

Cut bread into medium squares and set aside. Cube cheese in medium-sized pieces, cut crabmeat into large pieces and set aside. Spread bread, cheese and crabmeat in bottom of 8 x 10-inch buttered baking dish. Beat eggs, add mustard, salt, MSG and pepper. Pour egg mixture over bread, cheese and crabmeat. Refrigerate about 1 hour, or until ready to bake. Bake about 40 minutes at 350 degrees, until top is lightly browned. Serves ten-twelve.

CANDLEWYCK INN
Green Lane, Pennsylvania

Food editors have been very kind to the Candlewyck, and with good reason. I like to wander around the grounds by day, but nighttime is when Candlewyck can be seen at its most romantic. Candles provide the inn's main lighting, while the outdoor candle (a lighted silo) beckons to travellers.

OYSTERS CAPTAIN WHIDBEY

French bread, toasted	6 slices
oysters	36 medium
butter	6 tablespoons
Sauterne wine	1/2 cup
Hungarian paprika	1-1/2 teaspoons
sweet basil	1/4 teaspoon

Slowly saute oysters in butter, wine, paprika and basil, until just done, turning once. (Oysters are done when they feel firm to the touch.) Do not overcook. Spoon out on warm, toasted bread, skimming butter from liquid and pouring over oysters. Serve at once.

THE CAPTAIN WHIDBEY
Coupeville, Washington

From Whidbey Island, it is possible to see whales, some of them "a pretty good size," according to the innkeepers. I can't help but order seafood here, with the dining room overlooking Penn Cove. As I headed for the ferry that would take me back to the mainland, I knew this inn would become a welcome part of "Country Inns and Back Roads."

57

SHRIMP A LA NEWBURG

shrimp, cleaned and deveined	1-1/4 pounds
butter	3 tablespoons
salt	1/2 teaspoon
cayenne	a few grains
lemon juice	1 teaspoon
flour	1 teaspoon
cream	1/2 cup
egg yolks, slightly beaten	2
sherry wine	2 tablespoons

Cook shrimp 3 minutes in butter. Add salt, cayenne and lemon juice, cook 1 minute. Remove shrimp, put remaining butter in chafing dish. Add flour and cream, stirring until thickened. Add egg yolks, shrimp and wine and heat gently. Serves four.

CRANBURY INN
Cranbury, New Jersey

Newburg has long been a favored sauce for shrimp. This country restaurant treats it gently, with proper respect for the subtle blending of flavors. I like the peace of Cranbury, the village, as well as the inn. An easy drive both to New York and Philadelphia.

STUFFED FILET OF SOLE WITH CURRIED SHRIMP SAUCE

sole, filleted	8 3-1/2 ounce pieces
celery, finely chopped	1/2 cup
onion, minced	3 tablespoons
butter	3 tablespoons
bread crumbs, fine and dry	2 cups
poultry seasoning	1/2 teaspoon
parsley, chopped	1 tablespoon
crabmeat	3/4 cup
salt and pepper	to taste
Sauce:	
Maine shrimp (very small), raw, cleaned	1 cup
salted water	1 cup
butter	2 tablespoons
flour	2 tablespoons
curry powder	1/2 teaspoon or more
nutmeg	1/8 teaspoon
paprika	1/8 teaspoon
cream	1/2 cup
sherry wine	to taste

Saute celery and onion in butter about 4 minutes. Add bread crumbs, poultry seasoning, parsley, crabmeat, salt and pepper; blend well. Spread stuffing on fillet pieces; roll each loosely and secure with toothpick. Bake 30 minutes at 325 degrees.

Make sauce: Quickly boil shrimp in salted water; drain, reserving liquid. In top of double boiler, melt butter, blend in flour, curry powder, nutmeg, salt, paprika; stir until smooth. Slowly add cream and shrimp liquid; cook until smooth and thick. Add sherry to taste; gently stir in shrimp. Arrange 2 fish rolls for each serving. Ladle hot sauce over fish and garnish with parsley and lemon wedges. Serves four.

HOMEWOOD INN
Yarmouth, Maine

Honeymooners favor the Homewood's seaside location, its romantic geographical and historical setting, on the edge of Casco Bay.

BROILED SCALLOPS EN COQUELLE

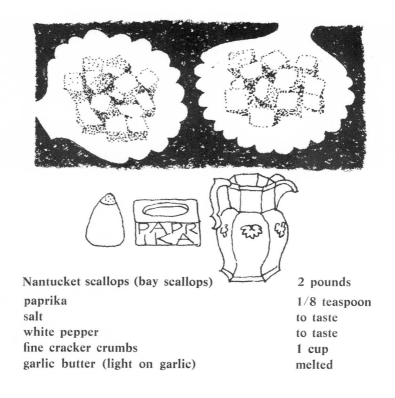

Nantucket scallops (bay scallops)	2 pounds
paprika	1/8 teaspoon
salt	to taste
white pepper	to taste
fine cracker crumbs	1 cup
garlic butter (light on garlic)	melted

Mix cracker crumbs, paprika, salt and pepper. Roll scallops in the mixture until well coated. Place in empty scallop shells or small casserole, one layer deep. Splash garlic butter over scallops and broil close to flame. Do not overcook.

JARED COFFIN HOUSE
Nantucket Island, Massachusetts

It takes a little extra effort to get to this inn, which stands stolidly on Nantucket Island. Whether by ferry or by air, a trek to the Coffin House is well worthwhile. I can think of no better way to initiate the palate than with Nantucket scallops.

STUFFED CLAMS A LA NORMANDE

clams, well scrubbed	18 large
shallots or scallions, chopped	2 tablespoons
mushrooms, finely chopped	3 tablespoons
butter	1 tablespoon
chives, minced	1-1/2 tablespoons
chervil or parsley, minced	1 teaspoon
bread crumbs, buttered	2 tablespoons
sherry wine	1 teaspoon
dry white wine	

Place clams in a kettle with just enough water to cover the bottom. Cover and cook over brisk flame until the shells open. Remove meat from shells, discarding rough neck part if using soft-shelled clams, and reserve shells. Chop clams finely; cook mushrooms in butter 1 minute. Blend clams, mushrooms, shallots, chives, chervil and bread crumbs. Add sherry and just enough dry white wine to moisten. Fill clam shells with this mixture, sprinkle with bread crumbs, and bake at 350 degrees until golden brown.

KIMBERTON COUNTRY HOUSE
Kimberton, Pennsylvania

In a light and airy dining room, overlooking an old mill pond complete with wheel, I lunched on beautiful food. These clams are stuffed with good seasonings and great care. Add a touch of country air and a dash of history (the inn is near Valley Forge) and the recipe will be complete.

BAKED STUFFED WHOLE BASS with CRABMEAT

whole bass	1 3-5 pounds
salt and pepper	to taste
onion, chopped	2 tablespoons
celery, chopped	1/4 cup
butter	1/2 cup
soft bread crumbs	2 cups
crabmeat, flaked	1 cup
parsley, chopped	1 tablespoon
milk	2 cups
onion, sliced	1 large
parsley sprigs and lemon	to taste

Wash bass and sprinkle inside and out with salt and pepper. Saute chopped onion and celery in butter, until lightly browned. Add bread crumbs, crabmeat, chopped parsley, salt and pepper, mixing well. Fill the fish with this mixture; tie or skewer fish together. Place in buttered pan with the milk; bake 45 minutes at 350 degrees. Garnish with onion rings, lemon and parsley.

LAKESIDE INN
Mount Dora, Florida

A nearly-New England community in the heart of Florida! The recipe is one of the prized personal possessions of chef-steward John Pillsbury.

OYSTER PIE

pie crust   **recipe for 1**

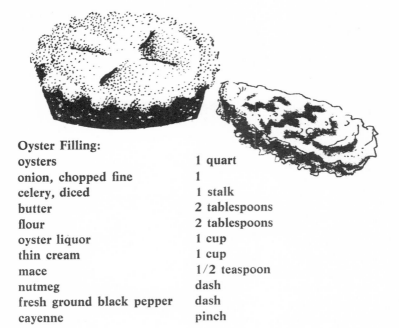

Oyster Filling:

oysters	1 quart
onion, chopped fine	1
celery, diced	1 stalk
butter	2 tablespoons
flour	2 tablespoons
oyster liquor	1 cup
thin cream	1 cup
mace	1/2 teaspoon
nutmeg	dash
fresh ground black pepper	dash
cayenne	pinch

Saute the onion and celery in butter until soft and golden. Stir in flour and seasonings. Add oyster liquor and let steep over hot water to blend seasonings. Gradually add cream, which must not be cooked too long as it may curdle. Add oysters to sauce about 5 minutes before serving and let them plump and heat through only until edges curl. Overheating may cause the sauce to become watery. Cut a circle of pastry the size of your serving dish (or make individual portions); bake crust separately. Fill dish with oysters and put on lid. Serve hot.

MARYLAND INN
Annapolis, Maryland

Here is a beautiful recipe typical of the many eastern shore dishes found at this inn which dates back to colonial Maryland.

COQUILLES SAINT-JACQUES with TOMATOES and MUSHROOMS

scallops	2 pounds
clam juice	1 cup
bay leaf	1 small
parsley	2 sprigs
green onions, chopped	3 tablespoons
shallots, chopped	1 tablespoon
dry white wine	1 cup
fresh, light cream	1/2 cup
butter	1/2 cup
flour	4 tablespoons
mushrooms (fresh), cut in pieces or whole, if small	2 cups
tomatoes (ripe), peeled, seeded and cut into pieces	3
buttered bread crumbs	
paprika	

Wash scallops to remove any sand, drain; cut into quarters or halves. Combine clam juice with bay leaf, parsley, onion and shallot; cook until reduced by half, strain, reserving liquid. Add white wine to liquid, heat; then add scallops. Cook gently for a few minutes, until scallops begin to turn white. Do not overcook. Remove scallops from liquid. Add cream to liquid, heat. Melt 4 tablespoons butter, add flour, blend into liquid. Cook over low heat, stirring constantly, until sauce is thick and smooth. Saute mushrooms in 4 table-spoons butter until no moisture remains; add tomatoes and cook until tomatoes are soft and thick. Mix sauce with scallops, tomatoes and mushrooms. Add salt if needed. Fill buttered scallop shells or individual casserole with mixture, sprinkle with bread crumbs, dust with paprika. Brown in hot oven or under broiler; garnish with chopped parsley.

MOHAWK INN
Old Forge, New York

This handsome dish from the Adirondack resort-inn is nearly a meal-in-one. It would be well complemented by a crisp, green salad and French or sourdough bread (fresh-baked, of course).

ELNOR WHITE'S SCALLOPED OYSTERS

dry bread crumbs	1/2 cup
coarse cracker crumbs	1/2 cup
butter, melted	5 tablespoons
oysters	1 pint
salt	1/2 teaspoon
pepper	1/8 teaspoon
nutmeg	1/8 teaspoon
parsley, chopped	2 tablespoons
mushroom soup	1 can

Combine bread crumbs, cracker crumbs and butter. Place half of mixture in greased casserole. Arrange oysters in layers, sprinkling each layer with seasonings. Pour mushroom soup over oysters; top with remaining crumbs. Bake 1 hour at 350 degrees. Serves four.

ROBERT MORRIS INN
Oxford, Maryland

Oxford, one of Maryland's oldest towns, is a perfect setting for an inn. Excellent food and accommodations make this a favorite stop. Wonderful, homemade desserts follow entrees like this one.

SUPERB RED SNAPPER

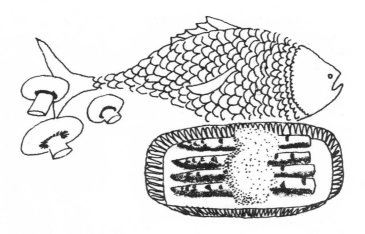

(For one portion)
snapper filet	6 to 8 oz.
asparagus	4 medium spears, cooked
hollandaise sauce	1/3 cup
seasoned mushroom caps	

Poach snapper filets until about half done or slightly firm. Place fish on top of cooked asparagus portions in a baking dish or pan. Top each filet with a generous portion of hollandaise sauce and bake in hot oven for 10 to 15 minutes depending on thickness of snapper filets. Place on a service platter and garnish with sauteed mushroom caps and chopped parsley.

NORMANDY INN
Louisville, Kentucky

The Normandy is a country restaurant in the city. The building which has been cleverly redesigned has a most interesting past. Fresh snapper prepared this way is one of the most frequently requested dishes on an extremely varied menu.

SHRIMP STUFFING

onion, minced	1/3 cup
celery, diced	1/2 cup
butter	1/4 cup
oyster cracker crumbs	2 cups, lightly packed
fresh shrimp, cleaned and cooked	1 cup

Cook onion and celery in butter over low heat until tender. Add cracker crumbs and let brown slightly. Add chopped shrimp and remove from heat. Stuff fish with this mixture and bake. To serve as main dish, instead of as a stuffing, eliminate chopped, cooked shrimp; top mixture with whole, raw shrimp and steam-bake. Will stuff a 5-pound fish, or the centers of 5 whole lobsters for broiling.

SPRINGSIDE INN
Auburn, New York

The lure of New York's lovely Finger Lakes region leads straight to the Springside. A professional theatre company, lush scenery, and much history are all at or near the inn.

FRUITS OF THE SEA

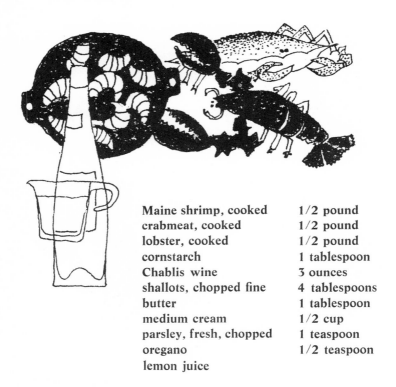

Maine shrimp, cooked	1/2 pound
crabmeat, cooked	1/2 pound
lobster, cooked	1/2 pound
cornstarch	1 tablespoon
Chablis wine	3 ounces
shallots, chopped fine	4 tablespoons
butter	1 tablespoon
medium cream	1/2 cup
parsley, fresh, chopped	1 teaspoon
oregano	1/2 teaspoon
lemon juice	

Saute shallots in butter in heavy saucepan. Add lobster, crabmeat and shrimp. Add cream and seasonings and simmer until hot but not boiling. Blend cornstarch and Chablis and stir until hot. Add lemon juice slowly. Serve on seasoned rice.

WHITEHALL INN
Camden, Maine

An inn on the Maine seacoast just has to show off its seafood, and this recipe is ideal for the purpose. Whitehall invites relaxation. Chess sets and jigsaw puzzles rest invitingly in secluded corners of the lobby and the small, antique-furnished lounging rooms. In 1912 Edna St. Vincent Millay first recited her poem, "Renascence," to a gathering at the inn.

POULTRY

BREAST OF CHICKEN ALGONQUIN

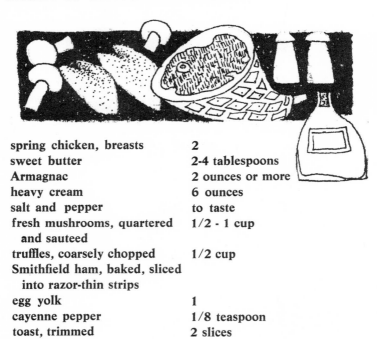

spring chicken, breasts	2
sweet butter	2-4 tablespoons
Armagnac	2 ounces or more
heavy cream	6 ounces
salt and pepper	to taste
fresh mushrooms, quartered and sauteed	1/2 - 1 cup
truffles, coarsely chopped	1/2 cup
Smithfield ham, baked, sliced into razor-thin strips	
egg yolk	1
cayenne pepper	1/8 teaspoon
toast, trimmed	2 slices

In chafing dish, saute chicken in butter until golden brown.
Pour Armagnac over chicken, ignite, then simmer. Slowly
add 4 ounces heavy cream; simmer 3-5 minutes. Season with
salt and pepper; add mixture of mushrooms and truffles.
Then add ham slices. Remove from heat. Lightly beat egg
yolk with 2 ounces heavy cream and cayenne pepper, then
stir into sauce and simmer 1 minute. Arrange toast on two
dinner plates; place breasts of chicken on toast and spoon
sauce over chicken. Serves two.

THE HOTEL ALGONQUIN
New York City, New York

I always feel my country heritage when I try to cope with New
York City. The Algonquin makes it possible to relax and enjoy
the ease and comfort of a country inn, even in that most bustling
of cities. This luxurious dish is best saved for company, or for
a very special, intimate dinner. It seems to demand candlelight
and soft music.

ROAST DUCKLING

duckling, quartered	**1 5-pound**
honey	**1/8 cup**
Cointreau	**3/4 ounce**
dry mustard	**1 teaspoon**
orange	**6 slices**
maraschino cherries	**4**

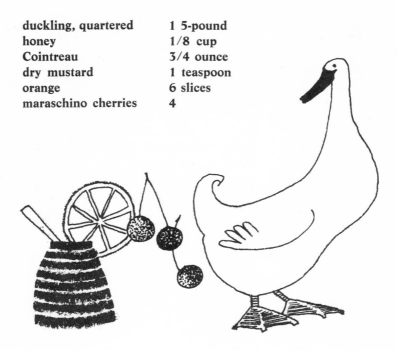

Place duck in broiler pan; combine honey, Cointreau and dry mustard. Brush duckling with mixture and broil until lightly browned. Remove from broiler and place in roasting pan, on rack. Bake about 3 hours at 350 degrees, until well done. Baste every 30 minutes and prick duckling as it roasts. Garnish with orange slice and cherry. Serves four.

BEEKMAN ARMS
Rhinebeck, New York

Another way to serve duckling, this time set off by a pungent, honeyed glaze. The village of Rhinebeck is set off by some of the Hudson Valley's loveliest back roads and restored homes and mansions.

ROAST YOUNG DUCKLING

ducklings	2 young
orange slices	
maraschino cherries	
Fruit Sauce:	
seedless raisins	1/2 cup
water	1 pint
cinnamon	1/4 teaspoon
allspice	1/8 teaspoon
orange juice	1 pint
pineapple, crushed	1/2 cup
maraschino cherry halves	1/2 cup
cornstarch	

Roast duckling in uncovered pan, 2 hours at 325 degrees. Remove from oven, allow to drain and cool several hours. When chilled and firm, use a serrated knife to cut along both sides of backbone; with your fingers, remove breastbone and small fiber bones. Leave wing and leg bone intact. About 20 minutes before serving, return to hot oven (425 degrees) to complete cooking. Serve with rice or rice pilaf; garnish with orange slices and maraschino cherries. Sauce: Soak raisins in water for about 1 hour. Add remaining ingredients, except cornstarch. Bring to a boil and simmer 30 minutes. Thicken with cornstarch until sauce is of syrupy consistency. May be made ahead of time and reheated in a double boiler. Serves four.

JOHN HANCOCK INN
Hancock, New Hampshire

Roast duck is one of my all-time favorite foods, and I never tire of discovering new ways to enjoy it. The John Hancock prepares it with a tasty spiced-fruit sauce. The inn is right in the middle of southern New Hampshire's Mt. Monadnock region; it is a favorite stop for big-city travellers as well as skiers and seekers after quiet vacations.

SOUTH SEAS CHICKEN

chicken breasts, boned	4
butter	4 teaspoons
tarragon	1 teaspoon
rosemary	1 teaspoon
egg, beaten lightly	1
bread crumbs	

Sweet and Sour Sauce:

onions, quartered	2
green pepper, cut in strips	1
butter	2 tablespoons
pineapple chunks, drained	1 can
pimento, drained, cut into strips	1 4-ounce can
vinegar	1/4 cup
pineapple juice	1/2 cup
cornstarch	2 tablespoons
water	1/2 cup

Place each breast between two sheets of waxed paper; pound until very thin. Remove paper and place a level teaspoon of butter in the middle of the chicken. Add tarragon and rosemary (¼ teaspoon for each breast). Roll the breast, folding over ends so entire roll is sealed. Roll in beaten egg and bread crumbs. Fry in deep fat 6-8 minutes at 325 degrees. Serve on bed of rice, covered with sweet and sour sauce. Decorate with sprig of watercress.

Sweet and Sour Sauce: Saute onions and green pepper in butter until onion is just transparent. Add pineapple, pimento, vinegar and pineapple juice. Bring to a boil; dissolve cornstarch in water; add to mixture and simmer, stirring, until sauce clarifies. Keep warm until ready to use.

HOMESTEAD INN
Greenwich, Connecticut

An altogether different way to treat breast of chicken, with a South-Sea island personality. The Homestead combines city sophistication with country charm.

DUCKLING A L'ORANGE

duckling, oven-ready   1 4-1/2—5-1/2 pound
salt

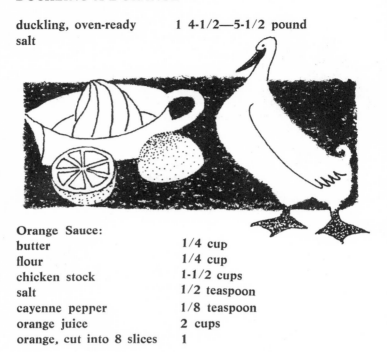

Orange Sauce:
butter	1/4 cup
flour	1/4 cup
chicken stock	1-1/2 cups
salt	1/2 teaspoon
cayenne pepper	1/8 teaspoon
orange juice	2 cups
orange, cut into 8 slices	1

Rub salt on duckling. Place on wire rack and roast 2-2-1/4 hours at 325 degrees, draining grease frequently. Remove from oven, cool; split in half, remove tail and set aside.

Sauce: Melt butter, blend in flour and add stock slowly. Add orange juice and orange sections. Before serving, roast duckling 12-15 minutes at 425 degrees, until golden brown. Pour hot orange sauce over duckling; garnish with orange slices. Serves four.

LONGFELLOW'S WAYSIDE INN
South Sudbury, Massachusetts

The 'oldest operating inn in America," a historic landmark, is midway between Boston and Worcester. The combination of orange and duck is also historic. This version is thoroughly delightful.

SOUR CREAM CHICKEN ENCHILADAS

boned chicken	3-pound can
mushrooms, bits and pieces	1-pound can
green chili (mild), chopped	2 4-ounce cans
garlic powder	to taste
salt and pepper	to taste
dried onions	1/2 cup
tortillas	2 packages
sour cream	3 pounds
cheddar cheese, grated	1 pound

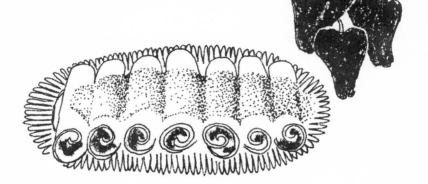

Mix the first six ingredients and heat gently so as not to burn. Dip tortillas in hot grease (quickly or they will be tough). Add chicken mixture to each tortilla and roll. Place on sheet pan, cover generously with sour cream and sprinkle with grated cheese. Bake at 450 degrees until cheese on top melts. May be prepared in advance and baked just before serving.

RANCHO ENCANTADO
Santa Fe, New Mexico

These are rather distinguished enchiladas. They are ideal for large crowds, easy to prepare ahead of time. The Rancho Encantado is truly enchanted, a ranch-inn that allows even its most famous guests near-total privacy and quiet.

CHICKEN A LA KING

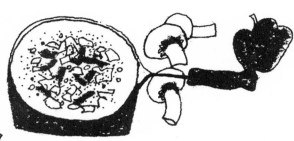

green pepper, diced	1 large
fresh mushrooms, sliced	2 cups
butter	6 tablespoons
flour	1/4 cup
milk, scalded	4 cups
chicken bouillon	1 teaspoon
egg shade color	
sherry wine	1 ounce
salt	to taste
pimentos, drained, sliced	1 4-ounce can
chicken, white and dark meat, cooked	4 cups

Saute green pepper and mushrooms in 2 tablespoons butter; set aside. Melt remaining 4 tablespoons butter, blend in flour, add milk; stir and cook slowly until of medium consistency. Add a drop or two of egg shade color, bouillon, sherry and salt. Stir in chicken, mushrooms, green pepper and pimento. Serve on toast or in patty shell.

ST. CLAIR INN
St. Clair, Michigan

I was half an hour from Detroit and yet I felt many more miles from the city as I savored the Scottish-style hospitality of "The Inn on the River." Chicken a la King is an old standby; the St. Clair's chef serves it with warm, freshly baked bread.

WESTERN BAR-B-QUE CHICKEN

fresh whole fryers	1-2
butter	1-2 sticks
onion, quartered	1
Sauce:	
butter	1/2 cup
lemon juice	1/4 cup
worcestershire sauce	1 tablespoon
prepared mustard	1 teaspoon
salt	1/2 teaspoon
peppers	1/8 teaspoon
chives or onions, finely chopped	3 tablespoons

Heat butter in saucepan; add remaining ingredients and blend thoroughly. Simmer 5 minutes. Makes about 3/4 cup. Put skewer through fryers; add butter and 1 onion (quartered)-1 stick of butter per fryer. Secure prongs and tie chicken on tightly. Place on spit; cook over slow fire, basting constantly. Makes a very moist chicken with unusual flavor.

TANQUE VERDE
Tucson, Arizona

Here is another Western specialty, also good company fare. At this charming ranch, I enjoyed my first real trip on horseback, soothed afterward by the inn's very welcome whirlpool baths.

CHICKEN A LA YANKEE CLIPPER

chicken, quartered	3 pounds
flour	1 cup
salt	1 teaspoon
paprika	1 teaspoon
cooking oil	to fill skillet 1" deep
celery	4 stalks
onion	2 medium
carrots	4
chicken stock	1 cup

Shake the pieces of chicken in a mixture of flour, salt and paprika. Fry in the skillet of hot oil until brown, remove the pieces from the skillet and place in a roasting pan. Cut the onions, celery, and carrots into small pieces and saute in the same oil used to fry chicken. Pour the sauteed vegetables and remaining oil over the chicken. Pour chicken stock over all and cover with foil. Cook in 300 degree oven for 1 1/2 hours. Before serving, pour off the liquid and thicken for a gravy.

YANKEE CLIPPER
Rockport, Massachusetts

Like its cousin just up the road a ways, the Yankee Clipper faces the sea at Rockport, Massachusetts. This is one of the dishes that the guests find most gratifying.

VEGETABLES

MINTY FRESH CARROTS

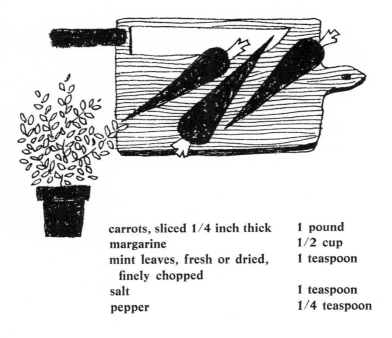

carrots, sliced 1/4 inch thick	1 pound
margarine	1/2 cup
mint leaves, fresh or dried, finely chopped	1 teaspoon
salt	1 teaspoon
pepper	1/4 teaspoon

Cook carrots in boiling, salted water until tender but not too soft; drain. Add remaining ingredients. Cook 3 minutes to blend seasonings. Serves four-six.

BOONE TAVERN HOTEL
Berea, Kentucky

One of the many wholesome and delightful dishes prepared by the tavern's fine cooks. Boone Tavern is owned by Berea College, an unusual institution that offers students training in many traditional crafts, as well as in academic subjects. The weaving and furniture industries are especially notable. Many items are available for purchase. Guests often enjoy the ancient game of skittles in the lobby, while awaiting dinner.

FRENCH FRIED ASPARAGUS

jumbo asparagus spears	1 #5 can
eggs, well beaten	4
milk	2 cups
bread crumbs	
flour	
deep fat or oil	

Mustard Sauce:

mayonnaise	1 cup
lemon juice	1/4 cup
prepared mustard	1 tablespoon

Drain asparagus and coat the spears with flour. Beat the eggs with the milk and dip the coated spears into the egg-milk mixture. Roll the spears in fine bread crumbs and allow to dry in layers, separated by paper toweling. Fry in deep fat (375 degrees) for 2 to 3 minutes or until golden brown. Serve with the Mustard Sauce: combine the above ingredients and keep warm in a small pan set in hot water.

CENTURY INN
Scenery Hill, Pennsylvania

Vegetables are a specialty at Century Inn, and this asparagus is no exception. The Insurrection Flag, from the Whiskey Rebellion, is just one of many antiques in the inn's extensive collection.

CLAYVILLE CARROTS

carrots, peeled and sliced	1 pound
butter or chicken fat	1/4 cup
onions, sliced	3 large
flour	1 tablespoon
chicken broth	1 1/4 cups
salt and pepper	to taste

Cook carrots in water until tender; drain. Saute onions in butter; add flour and chicken broth. Cook until slightly thick. Pour over carrots.

CLAYVILLE STAGECOACH STOP
Pleasant Plains, Illinois

The Clayville Stagecoach Stop is a restored community not far from New Salem, Illinois where Abraham Lincoln lived as a young man. In addition to Broadwell's Tavern, where Henry Clay stopped frequently, the restoration includes a pottery, a studio, a farmer's museum and a pioneer shop showing gardening, spinning, pottery and blacksmithing during the last century. The food is served in the country kitchen and is cooked by local farm ladies. These Clayville Carrots will send us all back to the farm.

CORNWALLIS YAMS

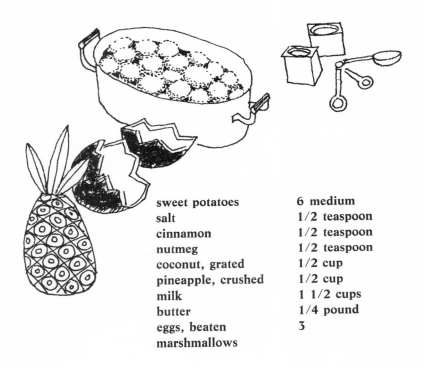

sweet potatoes	6 medium
salt	1/2 teaspoon
cinnamon	1/2 teaspoon
nutmeg	1/2 teaspoon
coconut, grated	1/2 cup
pineapple, crushed	1/2 cup
milk	1 1/2 cups
butter	1/4 pound
eggs, beaten	3
marshmallows	

Boil sweet potatoes, peel and mash them with a potato masher. Season with salt, cinnamon, nutmeg and butter. Add the beaten eggs, coconut, pineapple and milk and place in a greased casserole. Top with marshmallows and bake in a 350 degree oven until lightly browned.

COLONIAL INN
Hillsborough, North Carolina

It appears that Lord Cornwallis sat out the final days of the American Revolutionary War in Hillsborough, and because the spring season was so rainy and the roads became a mire, he ordered his soldiers to lay down the heavy stone walk which is still in existence in front of this inn. I love yams and this is a great recipe.

MAY'S TOMATO CASSEROLE

bread, sliced	1/2 loaf
tomatoes small, peeled, fresh or canned and drained	2 cups
salt	1/2 teaspoon
pepper	1/4 teaspoon
onion, chopped fine	1 tablespoon
milk	1-1/4 cups
eggs	3
New York cheese, grated	1 cup

Line bottom of buttered casserole with slices of bread. Spread tomatoes over bread; add salt, pepper, onion. Beat milk and eggs together and add; then add cheese. Bake 1 hour at 350 degrees.

HEMLOCK INN
Bryson City, North Carolina

This vegetable dish could become a whole meal, served with a salad and good bread. The Hemlock is right in the middle of the magnificent Great Smoky Mountains. Everything is easy-going and family-style.

SCALLOPED CABBAGE

cabbage, cut in 6-8 wedges	1 head
white sauce	1 cup
sharp cheese, shredded	1/2 cup
corn flake crumbs	1/4 cup
salt and pepper	to taste

Cook cabbage in boiling, salted water 10-12 minutes; drain. Heat white sauce and cheese together until cheese melts. Place cabbage in casserole; pour sauce over cabbage; shake corn flake crumbs over mixture. Add salt and pepper. Bake 30-35 minutes at 350 degrees, until hot and bubbly. Serves four-six.

NORTH HERO HOUSE
North Hero, Vermont

On North Hero Island, in Lake Champlain, I felt suspended between countries. The small country inn is almost equidistant from Montreal, Canada and Burlington, Vermont. Many land and water sports are available to guests.

STEWED TOMATOES

tomatoes	1 one-pound can
green pepper, shredded	1 small
onion, shredded	1 small
bacon	3 strips
salt and pepper	to taste
bread crumbs	1/2 cup

Fry bacon crisp; crumble in pan. Add pepper and onion; simmer until brown. Combine tomatoes with bacon, onions and pepper; cook until done, then add bread crumbs.

PARK VIEW INN
Berkeley Springs, West Virginia

The Park View has a slightly different view of tomatoes than most places do. I enjoyed the best of West Virginia cooking, including baked chicken, country ham and several kinds of vegetables. Just two hours from Washington, D.C., visitors can relax, enjoy the famous baths, or just bask in the warm inn atmosphere.

PLEASANT HILL SQUASH SOUFFLE

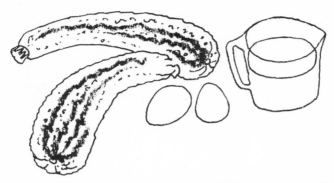

squash, yellow or zucchini	2 pounds
onion, sliced	1 medium
butter	3 tablespoons
eggs, beaten	3
cream of mushroom soup	1 can
salt	3/4 teaspoon
pepper	1/2 teaspoon
cracker crumbs	1/2-1 cup
parmesan cheese	1/4 cup

Cook squash and onion until tender; drain and mash. Fold in remaining ingredients; place in buttered casserole and top with cheese, then with cracker crumbs. Bake 30 minutes at 350 degrees.

INN AT PLEASANT HILL
Shakertown, Kentucky

As far as I know, this is the only restored historic village in the country in which visitors can spend the night in the original buildings. The 23 buildings are set in over 2000 acres of farmland. Furnishings are reproductions of Shaker originals, abounding in the simple beauty that marks all Shaker arts. Many Shaker specialties emanate from the kitchen.

ONION PIE

Crust:

flour	1-1/3 cup
salt	pinch
butter	1/4 pound
cream cheese	1 3-ounce package

Crust: Sift flour and salt together; work in butter and cream cheese thoroughly; dough will be crumbly, then lumpy and eventually, will form a single mass. Form a single ball from the crumbs, and set aside for 1/2 hour. Then roll out pastry 1/8 inch thick and line a 9-inch pie tin; prick bottom with fork. Pre-bake 15 minutes at 350 degrees. Cool and brush bottom with slightly beaten egg white.

Filling:

onions, chopped fine	1 pound
egg yolks	2
salt	1/2 teaspoon
pepper	1/2 teaspoon
flour	1 teaspoon
sour cream	1 cup
butter	1 tablespoon

Filling: Fry onions slowly in butter until golden brown; add salt and pepper. Mix sour cream with flour, pour over onions and bring to boiling-point, cool and stir in egg yolks slowly. Pour into crust and bake 20-25 minutes at 400 degrees.

STAFFORD'S-IN-THE-FIELD
Chocorua, New Hampshire

Here is a taste of Ramona Stafford's superb gourmet cooking. The inn offers warm weather relaxation and cold weather skiing.

HARVARD BEETS BURGUNDY

beets, tiny rosebud or shoestring	2 1-pound cans (4 cups)
cornstarch	2 tablespoons
sugar	1 cup
cloves, powdered	1/4 teaspoon
salt	1/8 teaspoon (dash)
wine, Burgundy or Claret	1 cup
wine vinegar	1/2 cup
butter or margarine	4 tablespoons

Drain beets, reserving liquid. Mix cornstarch, sugar, cloves and salt in saucepan; gradually add wine, vinegar, and 1/2 cup of beet juice, stirring until perfectly smooth. Stir over medium heat until mixture is thickened and clear. Add butter and beets; remove from heat, cover and let stand 30 minutes to blend flavors. Reheat before serving.

WELSHFIELD INN
Burton, Ohio

A nickelodeon plays old songs in the lobby of this country restaurant. The kitchen is one of the best-organized I have seen, and the food shows it, with special emphasis placed on the arrangement of food on each plate.

BRAISED TURNIPS

turnips, peeled	2 pounds
butter	2 tablespoons
sugar	1-2 teaspoons
meat stock	1 cup, scant
white sauce or Bechamel	1 cup or more
lemon juice	squeeze

Cook turnips slowly in butter. When they start to color and soften, sprinkle sugar all over and put in meat stock. Let simmer slowly uncovered, until soft. When stock has almost disappeared, put in white sauce made like a Bechamel, or an ordinary white sauce with a squeeze of lemon juice in it. Heat and serve.

WHITE HART INN
Salisbury, Connecticut

The rolling Litchfield Hills of Connecticut furnish many scenic drives. I like to travel to Salisbury via the road from Sharon.

RED CABBAGE WITH APPLES AND RED WINE

bacon, diced	3 slices
red cabbage, sliced thin	1 medium
red wine	1 cup
brown sugar	1/2 cup
apples, peeled and diced	2
cider vinegar	1/4 cup
salt	to taste

Cook bacon slowly in medium saucepan until brown and crisp. Remove from pan with slotted spoon. Place cabbage slices in pan with wine, sugar, apples, vinegar and salt. Cook uncovered at low heat until cabbage is tender, about 30 minutes. Sprinkle with bacon just before serving. Serves 5 or 6. (Good with rich meats, particularly pork.)

WILLIAMS INN
Williamstown, Massachusetts

On the campus of Williams College, the inn has hosted many a student over the years. The hospitality is warm and the food is good, and plentiful as well.

SALADS

PALM BEACH SALAD

avocado, sliced into 8 pieces	1 large
Belgian endive cut length-wise in 4 pieces	1 stalk
pineapple rings	4
watercress	8 sprigs
lettuce, leaf cup	4

Arrange lettuce leaf cup; put salad on this: place one piece of endive in center of pineapple ring. Arrange two slices of avocado beneath pineapple. Garnish with two sprigs of watercress. Serve with your favorite dressing. Serves four.

BRAZILIAN COURT HOTEL
Palm Beach, Florida

Dining on a patio amidst a profusion of flora that encircles a picturesque fountain – the quiet side of Palm Beach. Comfortable furnishings combine with the drama of the tropics to make this intimate hotel a place to stop and rest a while. In the heat of a Florida afternoon, this cool salad would be ideal.

CAULIFLOWER SALAD FARMHOUSE

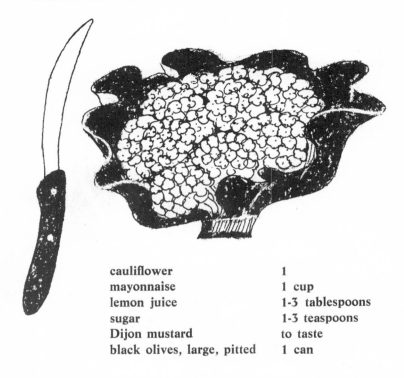

cauliflower	1
mayonnaise	1 cup
lemon juice	1-3 tablespoons
sugar	1-3 teaspoons
Dijon mustard	to taste
black olives, large, pitted	1 can

Core cauliflower and cut into small, bite-sized wedges. Cover with boiling water and allow to sit until cool; drain. Mix mayonnaise with lemon juice, sugar and mustard to taste. Dress salad and garnish with olives. Chill several hours or overnight in refrigerator.To add both interest and flavor, garnish with black sesame seed (called Kuro Goma) which can be purchased in any Japanese grocery store.

THE FARMHOUSE
Port Townsend, Washington

The Farmhouse would probably serve this for a summer's luncheon. Fall and Winter are devoted to a series of ethnic "seasons," with a different type of cuisine each month. I reached the inn by ferry, from Seattle to the Olympic Peninsula and Port Townsend. Getting there alone is a unique experience.

HOT BACON DRESSING

bacon	8 slices
sugar	1-1/2 cups
corn starch	3 teaspoons
salt	1/2 teaspoon
water	1/4 cup
vinegar	1/2 cup

Fry bacon until crisp, crumble and set aside. Mix dry ingredients, adding vinegar and water gradually; pour mixture over bacon and cook, stirring constantly until mixture thickens. Serve on endive, iceberg lettuce, dandelion greens, cucumbers, or on cabbage for hot slaw.

MOSELEM SPRINGS INN
Moselem Springs, Pennsylvania

Flaming gas lamps greet travellers to Moselem Springs, a historic restaurant near Reading and Allentown.

ZUCCHINI SALAD

zucchini, sliced thin	10 pounds
tomatoes, quartered	4 pounds
onions, sliced	3 pounds
salad oil	1 gallon
vinegar	1 1/2 quarts
salt and pepper	to taste
oregano	2 ounces
monosodium glutamate (Accent)	2 ounces

Put in stone jar for seven days. Turn daily. Serve.

OJAI VALLEY INN
Ojai, California

This resort-inn is a place for active, outdoor-loving people, with a wide variety of sports in an inviting setting. The salad, ice-cold, could be a fine refresher after a long, warm day on the golf course.

BREADS

BANANA BREAD

sugar	1 cup, scant
shortening	1/2 cup
bananas, very ripe, mashed fine	3 large
eggs, well beaten	2
flour	2 cups
salt	1/2 teaspoon
baking soda	1 teaspoon
baking powder	1 teaspoon
nuts, pecans or English walnuts, chopped	1/2 cup

Mix sugar, shortening and eggs. Add bananas and mix again. Lightly stir in flour, baking soda, salt and baking powder. Do not over mix. Stir in nuts; bake in greased bread pan about 50 minutes, at 350 degrees. Makes one loaf.

DE LA VERGNE FARMS
Amenia, New York

Comfortable pine furniture and the best of New England-style hospitality and cooking are to be found at this village inn. There is even a large wooden bowl, filled to the brim with shiny red apples, in the lobby. The inn is 190 years old, completely restored.

DILLY BREAD

yeast	2 cakes
warm water	1/2 cup
eggs	2
cottage cheese, small curd, warmed	2 1/2 cups
butter or margarine	2 tablespoons
shortening	4 tablespoons
salt	2 teaspoons
sugar	1/3 cup
baking soda	1/2 teaspoon
onion, minced	3 tablespoons
dill seed	1 teaspoon
dill weed	2 teaspoons
flour	4-5 cups

Dissolve yeast in warm water. Add everything except flour and mix well. Add flour for soft dough; let rise until doubled in bulk. Divide in two loaves, put in greased, round souffle casseroles. Let rise until doubled again. Bake 50 minutes at 350 degrees. Serve warm.

FARAWAY HILLS
Beverly, West Virginia

Deep in the West Virginia mountains, the adventurous traveller may encounter this rustic inn. Its setting is as poetic as its name, and the "dilly bread" is but one of countless culinary pleasures to be had here.

APPLE MUFFINS

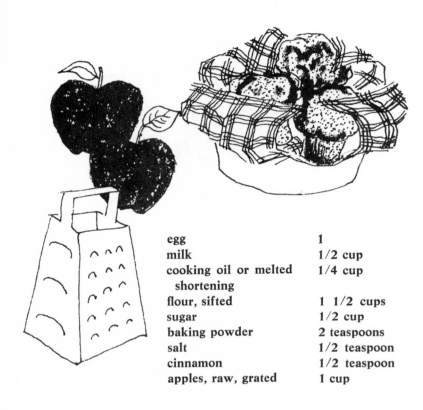

egg	1
milk	1/2 cup
cooking oil or melted shortening	1/4 cup
flour, sifted	1 1/2 cups
sugar	1/2 cup
baking powder	2 teaspoons
salt	1/2 teaspoon
cinnamon	1/2 teaspoon
apples, raw, grated	1 cup

Beat egg slightly, stir in milk and shortening. Sift together flour, sugar, baking powder, salt, cinnamon and add to egg mixture. Add apples. Pour into greased muffin tin. Bake 25-30 minutes at 400 degrees.

GRAVES MOUNTAIN LODGE
Syria, Virginia

Just two hours from Washington, D.C., with all its big-city sophistication, visitors to Graves Mountain Lodge can find the most serene of settings. Lucky guests reserve the rooms with fireplaces, especially when there's a chill in the air. The Blue Ridge foothills are within easy hiking distance.

POPOVERS

eggs, room temperature	4 large
fresh milk, room temperature	2 cups
flour, all-purpose, sifted	2 cups
salt	1/2 teaspoon
baking soda	1/8 teaspoon

Beat eggs with electric mixer at high speed, for 3 minutes or until thick and lemon-colored. Add 1 cup milk very slowly, beating at slowest speed until well mixed. Sift flour, salt and soda twice. Add these to egg mixture, beating at slowest speed until blended. Scrape sides of bowl; add rest of milk slowly, beating at medium speed for 2 minutes. Continue beating, at high speed, 5-7 minutes. Batter will be about the thickness of heavy cream and should be free of lumps. Generously grease muffin tins or custard cups. Fill about 2/3 full, with 3-4 inches of space between each cup. Bake 20 minutes at 425 degrees, on middle shelf of preheated oven. Reduce heat to 350 degrees and continue baking without opening oven, another 20 minutes. Serve at once. Makes approximately 10 large popovers.

JORDAN POND HOUSE
Seal Harbor, Maine

Popovers are a favorite of diners everywhere and a keynote of dinner at Jordan Pond House. To maintain the inn's tradition, serve them with mounds of fresh butter.

CRANBERRY COFFEE CAKE

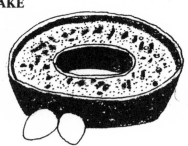

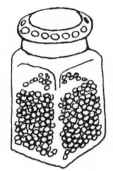

shortening	1/2 lb.
sugar	1 cup
eggs	2
flour	2 cups
baking powder	1 teaspoon
baking soda	1 teaspoon
salt	1/2 teaspoon
sour cream	1/2 pint
almond flavoring	1 teaspoon
cranberry sauce or jelly	1 7oz. jar
chopped nuts	

Topping:

sugar, confectioner's	3/4 cup
almond flavoring	1/4 teaspoon
water	

Mix ingredients as ordinary cake and spread one-half of batter in 8″ tube pan, then half the cranberry sauce or jelly. Add rest of batter then cranberry sauce. Sprinkle with nuts. Bake at 350 degrees for 55 minutes. Let cool 5 minutes and drizzle topping over cake.

Topping: Mix together confectioner's sugar, almond flavoring and enough warm water to bring to proper consistency.

KILMUIR PLACE
North East Margaree, Cape Breton, Nova Scotia

This Cranberry Coffee Cake is one of many delightful aromas created in Ross and Isabel Taylor's sumptuous farmhouse inn in the salmon fishing country of Cape Breton.

CALAS TOUS CHAUD

cooked rice	2 cups
yeast	1 cake
flour	4 cups
eggs	2
sugar	4 tablespoons
salt	1 1/2 teaspoons

Dissolve yeast in 1/2 cup warm water and stir into rice. Let rise overnight. Beat eggs until light, add salt and sugar and mix with rice mixture. Stir in the flour. Let rise for one hour, then drop by the tablespoon into medium-deep hot fat. Fry until brown. Drain and serve immediately with maple syrup or cane syrup. If preferred, sprinkle with confectioner's sugar and serve hot.

LAMOTHE HOUSE
New Orleans, Louisiana

Until I sat in Gertrude Munson's elegant dining room on a sunny morning enjoying "petit dejeuner," I really had not had the ultimate in Southern hospitality. The coffee is served from a two hundred-year-old handsome Sheffield urn and I was introduced to everyone at the table. This recipe is from a collection made by Mrs. Munson over many years. There are no short cuts here. Everything is done with patience, time and affection.

CRANBERRY BREAD

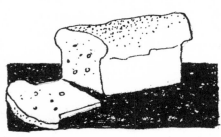

flour, all-purpose	2 cups
sugar	1 cup
baking powder	1 1/2 teaspoons
baking soda	1/2 teaspoon
orange juice	1 orange
salt	1/2 teaspoon
boiling water	
shortening	2 tablespoons
egg, well beaten	1
nuts, chopped	1/2 cup
cranberries, halved fresh, or canned, drained	1 cup

Sift dry ingredients. Add boiling water to shortening and orange juice to make 3/4 cup. Add to dry ingredients; then add egg, nuts and cranberries. Bake 1 hour at 325 degrees.

MELROSE INN
Harwich Port, Massachusetts

The cranberry bogs of Cape Cod are not far away. What better way to celebrate that fact than with fresh cranberry bread! Rolling lawns and abundant flowers surround the inn, which is only a 10-minute drive from Hyannis.

PUMPKIN BREAD

eggs	4
pumpkin, canned or fresh	1 3/4 cup
shortening, melted	3/4 cup
water	3/4 cup
sugar	3 cups
baking powder	1/2 teaspoon
baking soda	2 teaspoons
cloves, powdered	1/2 teaspoon
cinnamon, powdered	1 teaspoon
flour	3 1/3 cups
nuts (pecans), chopped	1 cup
salt	3/4 teaspoon

Combine eggs, pumpkin, shortening and water; Beat well. Set aside. Combine all dry ingredients, add nuts and mix well with moist ingredients. Grease 8 small loaf pans; fill 1/2 full. Bake 35-45 minutes at 350 degrees, until cake tester comes out clean. Makes 8 small loaves.

PATCHWORK QUILT COUNTRY INN
Middlebury, Indiana

The flat, Indiana farm country is quite a different scene from my native New England. The inn's name is perfect: it is indeed "patchwork quilt" country. Hot mulled cider might accompany this bread at the beginning of an unbelievable meal. Homemade soup bubbles away in a large iron pot on the hearth, and appetizers — of which I counted over thirty — are served buffet style. To top it off, I had to decide which of Arletta Lovejoy's fantastic desserts to sample!

OATMEAL MUFFINS

oatmeal	2 cups
sour cream	1 pint
brown sugar	2 cups
butter, softened	2/3 cup
eggs	4
flour, all-purpose	2 cups
baking powder	2 teaspoons
baking soda	1 teaspoon
salt	1 teaspoon

Mix oatmeal with sour cream and let them soak. Cream sugar and butter together. Add eggs one at a time; stir in oatmeal and sour cream mixture. Sift together flour, baking powder, soda and salt, and stir into the mixture. Spoon into greased muffin tins and bake about 25 minutes at 375 degrees. Makes two dozen.

RABBIT HILL INN
Lower Waterford, Vermont

After my experience, I would strongly urge visitors to include a Friday night in their plans for Rabbit Hill. That is Clambake night, when the traditional clambake fare is supplemented by a choice of steak or lobster. These oatmeal muffins usually appear at breakfast. Any time, I like the fresh flowers, candles, the Currier and Ives prints, and the other personal touches that make Rabbit Hill special.

DESSERTS

BLUEBERRY BOOPE BOMBE

butter, sweet	1 pound
sugar	2 cups
eggs, separated	12
chocolate, unsweetened, melted	4 ounces
vanilla extract	1 teaspoon
pecans, chopped	1 cup
ladyfingers, split	2 large packages
bourbon	1 cup
heavy cream, whipped	1 1/2 cups

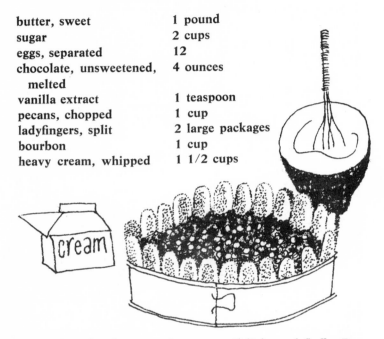

Cream together butter and sugar until light and fluffy. Beat egg yolks until light, and beat into creamed mixture. Beat chocolate into mixture, and add vanilla and pecans. Beat egg whites until stiff but not dry; fold into other ingredients. Line a 10-inch springform pan around the side and bottom, with split ladyfingers that have been quickly dipped in bourbon. (Finish up any leftover bourbon as you wish!) Fill pan with mixture; chill as long as possible—overnight is best; may be lightly frozen to speed the chilling process. To serve, remove sides of pan and decorate with whipped cream. Serves sixteen.

BLUEBERRY HILL FARM
Brandon, Vermont

This is one of the richest and most fanciful desserts I've encountered anywhere. Cross-country skiing is the inn's trademark, and children join in as enthusiastically as the adults. Martha Clark's wonderful cooking also appeals to guests of all ages.

110

ORANGE NUT CAKE

butter or margarine	3/4 cup
sugar	1 1/2 cups
eggs	2
flour	2 cups
salt	1/2 teaspoon
vanilla extract	1/2 teaspoon
nuts, chopped	1/2 cup
raisins	1/2 cup
orange rind, grated	1/2 orange
sour cream, commercial type	1 cup
baking soda	1 teaspoon

Syrup:

sugar	1/2 cup
orange juice	1/2 cup
brandy (optional)	1 ounce

Cream shortening and sugar; add eggs and mix until smooth. Sift flour and salt together. Add soda to sour cream. Add flour and cream alternately to mixture. Add orange rind, nuts, raisins, and vanilla. Bake in greased and floured tube pan, about 45 minutes at 375 degrees. Remove outer rim and baste with syrup while cake is hot; use a spoon, covering top and sides until all liquid is absorbed. (Cake **must** be hot!)

BOULDERS INN
New Preston, Connecticut

Jane Lowe says this is husband Dick's most often-requested recipe and adds,"We have been somewhat choosy about sharing it. . ." At this year-round resort-inn, they're into the fourth generation of innkeeping. Specialties such as the spectacular orange nut cake might be part of the reason.

BRANDIED APPLE COBBLER

apples, greening	2 1/2 pounds
lemon juice	1 tablespoon
lemon rind	1/4 teaspoon
sugar, white	3/8 cup
sugar, brown	3/8 cup
cinnamon	1/2 teaspoon
salt	1/8 teaspoon
brandy	2 ounces

Combine apples, lemon juice and brandy; spread in pan, 14x 9x12. Mix sugar and spices and sprinkle over apples.

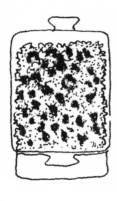

Topping	
brown sugar	1/2 pound
cinnamon	1 teaspoon
white sugar	1/2 pound
butter	1/4 cup
shortening	3/4 cup plus 2 tablespoons
flour	2 -1/4 cups
salt	1/2 teaspoon
baking powder	1 teaspoon
Zwieback crumbs	1 cup
brandy	2 ounces

Topping: Cream butter, shortening and brandy well. Add sugar and mix thoroughly. Combine flour, salt, baking powder, cinnamon and zwieback crumbs; add to mixture and mix well. Spread in pan, over apple mixture; bake 30-40 minutes at 375 degrees.

THE BULL'S HEAD INN
Cobbleskill, New York

Apple cobbler is an old standby. The Bull's Head recipe adds several unusual flourishes, not the least of them a goodly bit of brandy.

CRANBERRY CRUNCH PIE

whole cranberries, washed	3 cups
sugar	3/4 cup
walnuts, chopped	1/2 cup
margarine	1/2 cup (1 stick)
sugar	1 cup
eggs, beaten	2
flour	1 cup

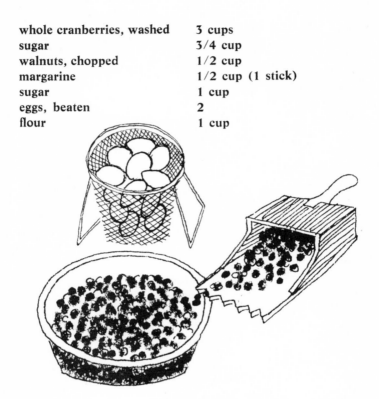

Spread cranberries in greased 9-inch pie plate; cover with sugar and nuts. Melt margarine, mix in sugar, eggs and flour. Beat until batter is smooth; pour over cranberry mixture and bake 1 hour at 325 degrees. Turn upside down and serve warm with vanilla ice cream or whipped cream. Recipe freezes well. Serves eight.

CRAIGVILLE INN
Craigville, Massachusetts

A church-operated family resort, the inn is near some of Cape Cod's loveliest beaches. The recipe makes appropriate use of one of the Cape's most delectable resources—its cranberry crop.

POTATO CAKE

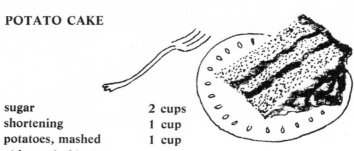

sugar	2 cups
shortening	1 cup
potatoes, mashed (the real thing)	1 cup
eggs, separated	4
flour	2 cups
cocoa	3 tablespoons
baking powder	2 teaspoons
cinnamon	1 teaspoon
nutmeg	1 teaspoon
cloves, ground	1 teaspoon
milk	3/4 cup

Frosting:	
butter	2 tablespoons
peanut butter	1/2 cup
powdered sugar, sifted	3 1/2 cups
milk	6 tablespoons, approximately
dates, pitted	enough to decorate

Cream sugar with shortening. Add potatoes; stir in egg yolks. Sift dry ingredients; add milk alternately with flour mixture; fold in egg whites. Pour into three 9-inch layer cake pans. Bake 20 minutes at 350 degrees, until toothpick comes out of center clean and cake is away from side of pan. Frost with Peanut Butter Frosting: blend butter with peanut butter; sift in sugar, adding enough milk to make it soft enough to spread. Decorate with pitted dates.

HERITAGE HOUSE
Little River, California

Sixty-foot cliffs overlooking the ocean near the delightful inn. The guest houses are antique-furnished and some even have sod roofs.

ICE CREAM PUFFS WITH HOT MAPLE SAUCE

butter or margarine	1/2 cup (1 stick)
water, boiling	1 cup
flour, all-purpose, sifted	1 cup
salt	1/4 teaspoon
eggs	4

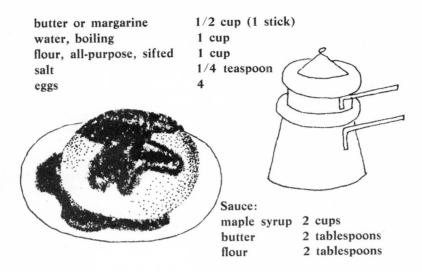

Sauce:

maple syrup	2 cups
butter	2 tablespoons
flour	2 tablespoons

Melt butter in boiling water; add flour and salt all at once, stirring vigorously. Cook and stir until mixture forms a ball that does not separate. Remove from heat, cool slightly. Add eggs one at a time, beating after each until smooth. Drop by heaping tablespoons, three inches apart on greased cookie sheet. Bake 15 minutes at 450 degrees, then 25 minutes at 325 degrees. Remove from oven and split puffs. Turn oven off, put cream puffs back in to dry for about 20 minutes. Cool on rack. Makes 15 large or 18 small. Stuff with vanilla ice cream; wrap and store in freezer until ready to serve.

Sauce: Melt butter, blend in flour, add syrup. Cook slowly in double boiler until thick. Makes two cups sauce. Heat thoroughly and pour over frozen cream puffs.

KEDRON VALLEY INN
South Woodstock, Vermont

This is a delicious way to serve real Vermont maple syrup. Guests often spend much of their time here on horseback, enjoying the scenic trails.

POMPADOUR PUDDING

milk	1 quart
sugar	3/4 cup
cornstarch	2 tablespoons
salt	1/3 teaspoon
eggs, separated (yolks)	3
vanilla extract	2 teaspoons

Topping:

chocolate, unsweetened	2 squares
sugar	3/4 cup
milk	4 tablespoons
(egg whites)	

Scald milk, add sugar, cornstarch and salt and cook for 15 minutes. Add egg yolks and cook 5 minutes; add vanilla and fill 6-ounce size custard cups three-fourths full. Topping: melt chocolate, add sugar and milk. Beat the three egg whites until stiff and dry; add to chocolate mixture. Place topping on pudding, dividing among cups until level. Pre-heat oven to 325 degrees; bake 45 minutes in pan filled with water.

LARCHWOOD INN
Wakefield, Rhode Island

An inn near the famous Rhode Island beaches, the Larchwood has many Scottish touches. This pudding fits in well with the Scottish motif.

CRANBERRY PUDDING

cranberries	1 can
molasses	1/2 cup
baking soda, in 1/2 cup hot water	2 teaspoons
flour	1 1/2 cups

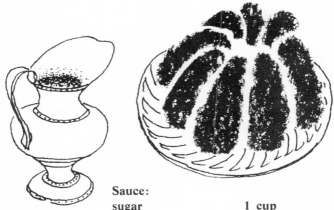

Sauce:	
sugar	1 cup
butter	1/2 cup (1 stick)
heavy cream	1/2 cup
rum (dark preferred)	2 tablespoons

Mix first five ingredients well. Pour in mold and steam 2 hours. Serve warm with sauce. Sauce: cream butter and sugar, add cream; melt in double boiler. Add rum; pour over pudding. Serves six-eight.

NEW ENGLAND INN
Intervale, New Hampshire

Here is another tasty way to use New England cranberries. At the inn, I worked up a ravenous appetite with an early morning swim in the fresh, mountain air. In colder weather there is ample skiing in the nearby White Mountains.

RALPH WALDO EMERSON PIE CRUST

flour	3 cups
lard (yellow if possible)	1/2 pound
water	1/3 cup
vinegar	1 tablespoon

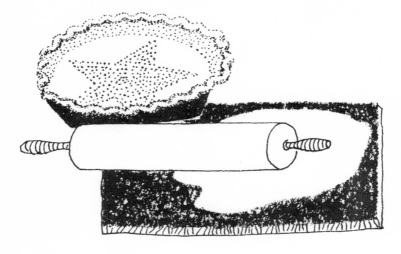

Cut flour and lard with a pastry blender until it resembles corn meal. Use light strokes; don't mash. Add water and vinegar, turning the mixture with a spoon to spread the water. Form into dough by hand and divide into three balls. Roll out on a well-floured pastry board to shape of pie tin. It will be very fragile; fold in half and move with care. Makes one 2-crust pie and one shell or three 1-crust pies.

RALPH WALDO EMERSON
Rockport, Massachusetts

Until I saw this recipe I hadn't thought of yellow lard in many years. Among the other interesting ingredients is the tablespoon of vinegar. The Ralph Waldo Emerson overlooks the ocean at Rockport. It is a most enjoyable experience to climb among the rocks and beaches and do the shops in this Massachusetts sea-coast village on the shores of Cape Ann.

HEAVENLY BREAD AND BUTTER PUDDING

white bread	12 slices
golden raisins	1/2 cup
currants	1/2 cup

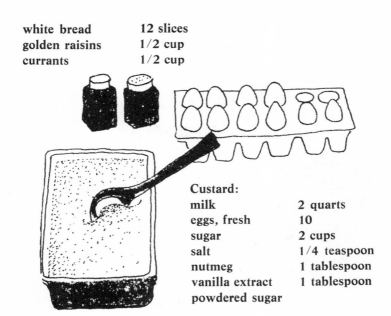

Custard:

milk	2 quarts
eggs, fresh	10
sugar	2 cups
salt	1/4 teaspoon
nutmeg	1 tablespoon
vanilla extract	1 tablespoon
powdered sugar	

Butter bottom and sides of a 3-quart, oblong Pyrex baking dish. Remove crusts from bread and cut slices diagonally. Place in casserole slightly overlapping; set aside. Prepare custard: combine all ingredients except milk, beating well; stir in heated milk. Pour over bread slowly, so as not to disturb bread. Place in pan of water and bake until custard is firm, at 400 degrees. Remove pudding from water; dust with powdered sugar. Place under broiler until sugar melts. Serves twelve-sixteen.

SNOWBIRD MOUNTAIN LODGE
Robbinsville, North Carolina

Perched high in the Great Smokies, this rough-hewn inn sits 1,000 feet above an ice-clear lake. A birder's paradise; the mammoth fireplace guards against even the summer evening's chill. Hikers' ravenous appetites are met with hardy fare, topped off with the likes of this "heavenly" pudding.

ENGLISH TRIFLE

lady fingers	6
raspberry jam	
sherry wine	6 tablespoons
bananas, sliced	2
peaches, canned, sliced	1 can
eggs, separated	2
castor sugar	1 ounce
milk	1/2 pint
raspberry gelatin	1 package
double cream	1/2 pint

Split ladyfingers in half; sandwich with jam. Arrange in base of serving dish and soak in sherry. Add sliced bananas and peaches. Make gelatin and pour on top, leave to set. Blend together egg yolks and sugar; warm milk and pour over the egg mixture. Stir well; return to pan and cook over low heat. Do not allow to simmer. When thick enough to coat back of a wooden spoon, remove from heat. Strain over lady fingers and leave to set. Just before serving, whip cream with egg whites until it forms soft peaks; spread over trifle. Top with cherries. Serves six.

STAGECOACH HILL INN
Sheffield, Massachusetts

A dessert not to be trifled with—and a favorite of guests at Stagecoach Hill, a British inn in the Berkshires. Summer festivals and winter skiing are close by.

LEMON FROMAGE WITH STRAWBERRIES

eggs, whole	3
egg yolks	2
sugar	1/2 cup
lemon rind, grated	1 lemon
unflavored gelatin	1 tablespoon
lemon juice	1/4 cup
heavy cream	2 cups
strawberries, washed and sweetened to taste	1 pint

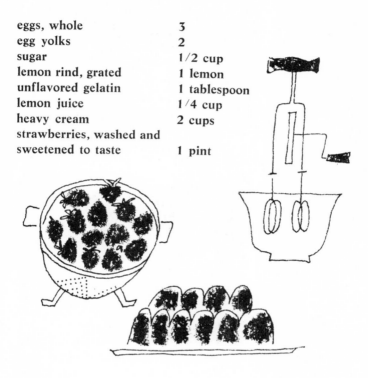

Beat eggs and yolks until lemon-colored and frothy, gradually adding sugar and continuing to beat until thickened. Add rind. Combine gelatin and lemon juice in heatproof measuring cup; place over hot water; stir until gelatin dissolves. Gradually add to egg and lemon mixture. Pour into a one-quart mold and chill 4 hours. Unmold and serve with strawberries. Serves six.

THREE VILLAGE INN
Stony Brook, New York

I find the subdued atmosphere especially attractive second only to the fine food at this village inn on Long Island's historic north shore.

BLUEBERRY CREAM PIE

blueberry pie filling	1 can
sour cream, commercial type	1 1/2 cups
pie crust, baked and cooled	1 9-inch crust

Fill crust by dropping filling and sour cream by heaping teaspoonfuls, in alternating layers until filling is used up. Using a spatula or table knife, gently swirl until a marbleized appearance is achieved. Refrigerate 1 hour before serving. May be served with sour cream or whipped cream topping.

WELLS INN
Sistersville, West Virginia

The Wells is a restored Victorian village inn, with much charm and fine cuisine. A good, light crust would best show off this pretty pie.

THIRST QUENCHER

orange juice, fresh	1 cup
pineapple juice, unsweetened	1 cup
lemon juice, fresh	1/4 cup
maraschino cherry juice	1/4 cup
dry ginger ale	1 cup
honey	2 tablespoons
French vanilla ice cream	1 pint
maraschino cherries, sliced	2 tablespoons

Mix fruit juices and ginger ale, add honey and mix well. Chill thoroughly. Add ice cream and stir until blended. Serve in frosted glasses topped with a sprinkling of cherry slices. Makes 1 1/2 quarts.

THE WHISTLING OYSTER
Ogunquit, Maine

The "Thirst Quencher" could be an appetizer or an afternoon refresher, as well as a dessert. Ogunquit is one of my favorite haunts, with its artists, writers, theatre and shops, its rugged cliffs and rolling sea.

BANANA WHIP AND MACAROONS

bananas, overripe	6-8
sour cream, thick	1 cup
sugar	to taste
fresh nutmeg	a grating

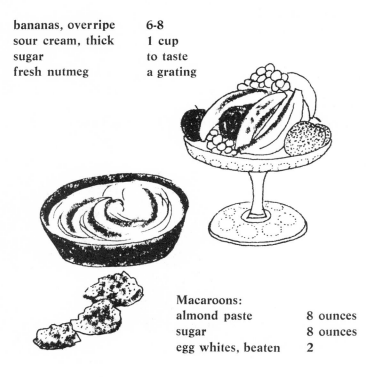

Macaroons:

almond paste	8 ounces
sugar	8 ounces
egg whites, beaten	2

Mash bananas and mix with sour cream and sugar; put into pudding dishes and top with nutmeg. Serve with macaroons: mix all ingredients until *very* smooth. Drop by teaspoonfuls on buttered brown paper on cookie sheet. Bake 30 minutes at 325 degrees. Cool slightly and wet paper to remove.

WHITE ROCK MANOR
Fayetteville, Pennsylvania

I was lucky enough to be there for White Rock Manor's gala plantation-style dinner, served on Friday, Saturday and Sunday nights. All six courses were outstanding. I even recovered in time to view the attractive surrounding landscape.

HOT FRESH STRAWBERRIES AU SABAYON

strawberries, washed, hulled and dried	3 pints
water	1 quart
sugar	1 3/4 cups
strawberry coloring	1 teaspoon
lemon, thin skin removed	1
vanilla extract	dash

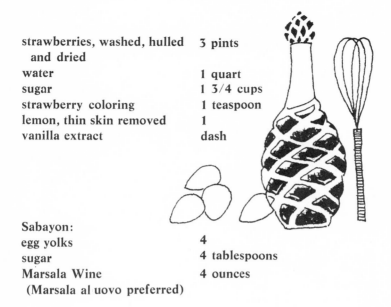

Sabayon:	
egg yolks	4
sugar	4 tablespoons
Marsala Wine (Marsala al uovo preferred)	4 ounces

Put water, sugar, vanilla, lemon skin in shallow saucepan and boil about 5 minutes. Remove lemon skin. Add berries, cover and bring to brisk boil for about 1 minute. Drain in a colander; spread in shallow serving bowl and keep warm while making the sabayon: put egg yolks, sugar and wine in stainless steel bowl; beat with whisk until frothy. Place bowl in boiling water and beat constantly until mixture is foamy and will stand at a peak. Spread over hot strawberries and serve. Lady fingers or small, soft cakes may be served to accompany. Serves six.

THE YANKEE PEDLAR
Holyoke, Massachusetts

I can't think of a more exciting way to present fresh strawberries. This aristocratic dish follows the very substantial seafood, beef and fowl entrees. Students, parents and faculty from the several nearby colleges and preparatory schools are among the inn's most appreciative visitors.

INDEX OF INNS

General Lewis (King Crabmeat Dip), 15
Golden Lamb (Stuffed Pork Chops), 44
Graves Mountain Inn (Apple Muffins), 102
Green Mountain (Cheese Soup), 27

John Hancock (Roast Young Duckling), 72
Hemlock Inn (May's Tomato Casserole), 84
Harborside Inn (Kale Soup), 28
Heritage House (Potato Cake), 114
Homestead Inn (South Seas Chicken), 73
Homewood Inn (Stuffed Filet of Sole), 59
Hovey Manor (Chinese Green Pepper Steak), 45

Inverary Inn (Seafood Chowder), 29

Jared Coffin House (Broiled Scallops), 60
Jordan Pond House (Popovers), 103
Lord Jeffery (Farmer's Omelet), 37

Kedron Valley Inn (Ice Cream Puffs), 115
Kilmuir Place (Cranberry Coffee Cake), 104
Kilravock Inn (Endives and Ham in Mornay Sauce), 46
Kimberton Country Inn (Stuffed Clams), 61

Lakeside Inn (Baked Stuffed Bass), 62
Lamothe House (Calas Tous Chaud), 105
Larchwood Inn (Pompadour Pudding), 116
Leelanau Homestead (Cocktail Sauce), 17
Lincklaen House (Hollandaise Sauce), 18
Longfellow's Wayside Inn (Duckling a l'Orange), 74
Lyme Inn (Wiener Schnitzel), 47

Maryland Inn (Oyster Pie), 63
Melrose Inn (Cranberry Bread), 106
Mohawk Inn (Coquilles St. Jacques), 64
Morgan House (Veal Stew), 48
Robert Morris Inn (Scalloped Oysters), 65
Moselem Springs Inn (Hot Bacon Dressing), 96
Mountain View Inn (Hungarian Beef Goulash), 49

New England Inn (Cranberry Pudding), 117
New London Inn (Yankee Pot Roast), 50
Normandy Inn (Superb Red Snapper), 66
North Hero House (Scalloped Cabbage), 85
Nu-Wray Inn (Pear Relish), 19

Old Club (Ham and Macaroni Casserole), 38
Old Red Mill (Seafood Stuffed Tomatoes), 20
Ojai Valley Inn (Zucchini Salad), 97

Park View Inn (Stewed Tomatoes), 86
Patchwork Quilt Country Inn (Pumpkin Bread), 107
Pleasant Hill Inn (Squash Souffle), 87
Pump House Inn (Alpine Cheese Soup), 30

Rabbit Hill (Oatmeal Muffins), 108
Rancho de los Caballeros (Chili con Carne), 51
Rancho Encantado (Sour Cream Chicken Enchiladas), 75
Red Lion Inn (Cold Cucumber Soup), 31

Sagebrush Inn (Chile Rellenos), 21
St. Clair Inn (Chicken a la King), 76
Sawmill Farm (Grammy's Tomato Juice), 16
1740 House (Chilled Avocado Soup), 32
Snowbird Mountain Lodge
    (Heavenly Bread and Butter Pudding), 119
Springside Inn (Shrimp Stuffing), 67
Stafford's Bay View (Squash Bisque), 33
Stafford's-in-the-Field (Onion Pie), 88
Stagecoach Hill (English Trifle), 120
Sutter Creek (Scrambled Eggs), 39
Swiss Hutte (Sweetbreads des Gourmets), 52

Tanque Verde (Western Barbecued Chicken), 77
Three Village Inn (Lemon Fromage with Strawberries), 121

Wayside Inn (Peanut Soup), 34
Welshfield Inn (Harvard Beets Burgundy), 89
Wells Inn (Blueberry Cream Pie), 122
Whistling Oyster (Thirst Quencher), 123
White Hart Inn (Braised Turnips), 90
Whitehall Inn (Fruits of the Sea), 69
White Rock Manor (Banana Whip and Macaroons), 124
Williams Inn (Red Cabbage with Apples and Wine), 91

Yankee Clipper (Chicken a la Yankee Clipper), 78
Yankee Pedlar (Hot Fresh Strawberries au Sabayon), 125

INDEX